SISTERS OF GRIT

Voices of Twelve Remarkable American Women

BARBARA M. WOHLFORD

Please direct all correspondence and book orders to:
bonwo634@comcast.net

Library of Congress Control Number 2018943796
ISBN 978-0-692-11400-1

Published for the author by
Otter Bay Books, LLC
3507 Newland Road
Baltimore, MD 21218-2513

www.otter-bay-books.com

Printed in the United States of America

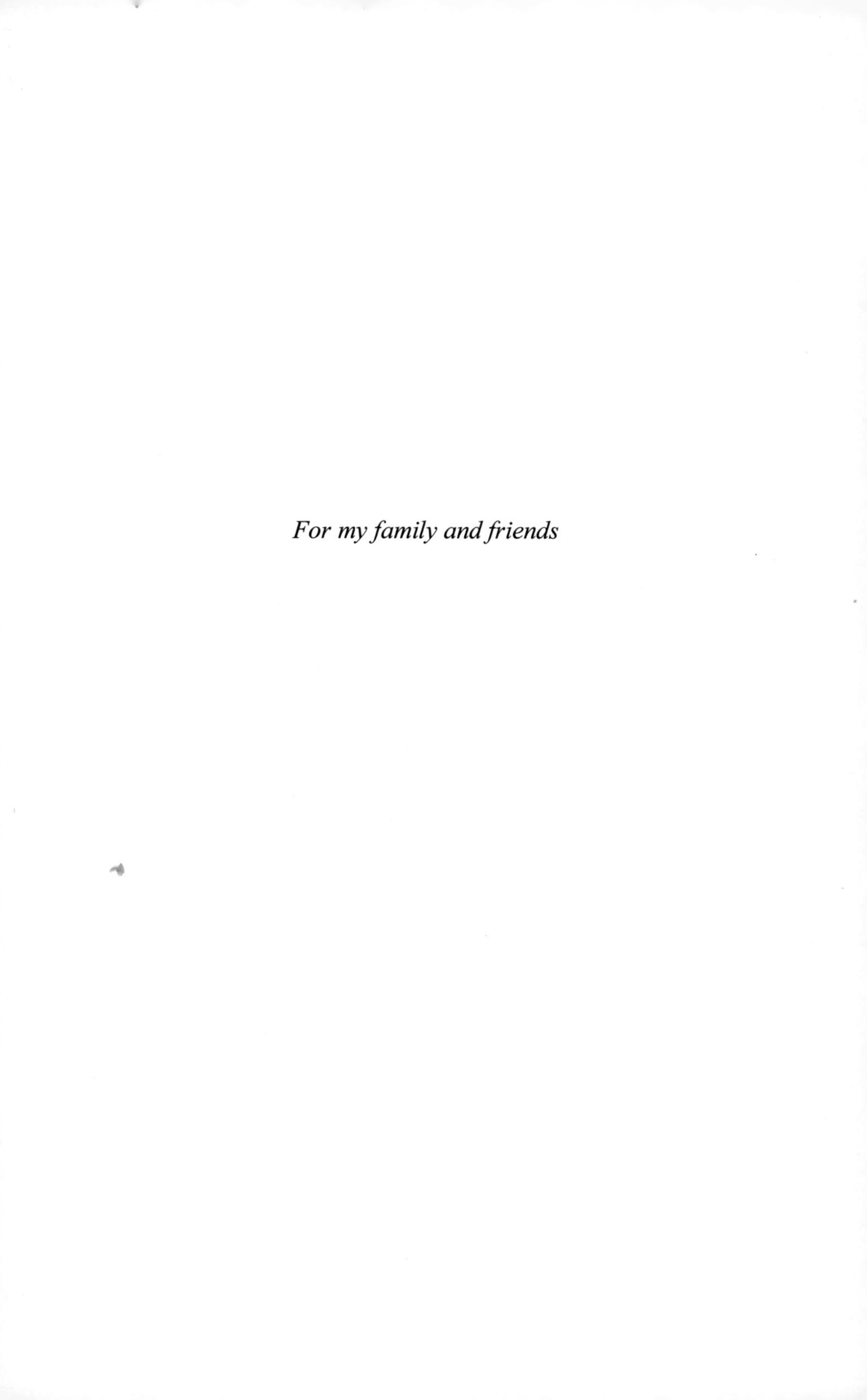

For my family and friends

CONTENTS

ACKNOWLEDGEMENTS

I am indebted to a number of people for their generous assistance throughout this project. Many, many thanks to my Jill-of-all-trades, Maria Kelly. Maria, you were invaluable as proof-reader, editor, fact-checker, supporter and most importantly, dear friend. Thanks also to my fellow writers of the Writers Workshop at the Osher Lifetime Learning Institute (OLLI) sponsored by George Mason University. Special hugs go to Ed Stadtler, Beth Ticknor, Ralph Greenwood and June Baek. These four wonderful writers were with me from the beginning of this project and listened patiently while I wrote about "still more women." I value your thoughtful comments, insights and encouragement.

There probably would never have been a book at all without the support of my "tech team." I am forever grateful to my grandson Ryan Benson who corrected my frequent computer goof-ups and answered my repeated computer questions with never-failing good humor and patience. My son, Scott Benson, and daughter-in-law, Melissa Benson, spent many hours helping me format this manuscript and intervened when I threatened to commit "computercide." Thank you Ryan, Scott, and Melissa.

Heartfelt thanks are extended to the many people who suggested names as possible candidates for inclusion in this book and to my son Glenn and daughter-in-law Lillian Benson for telling me about Grandma Gatewood and the Lady of Cofitachequi. Your support and encouragement were invaluable.

I received much welcome support from my son Donn Benson and from the cadre of friends who took the time to read all or parts of the manuscript. I am indebted to all of you and can't thank you enough.

I am grateful to Ann Hughes and Kate Boyer of Otter Bay Books for their expertise, advice and professionalism in helping bring my project to fruition.

INTRODUCTION

Throughout the ages, the achievements of women, all too frequently, have been unsung, ignored, downgraded and dismissed. The intention of *Sisters of Grit* is to help rectify this state of affairs by recognizing and applauding the accomplishments of twelve remarkable women. The women spotlighted are just a tiny representation of the plethora of exceptional women whose stories deserve to be told. Found on these pages are the voices of an artist and an actress, a scientist and a spy, and ordinary women who accomplished extraordinary feats that have left signature and important imprints on the American story. Yet, their names are recognized by very few. The twelve women showcased come from all walks of life. Their ages span the gulf between teenager and septuagenarian. They represent diverse ethnicities and dissimilar economic backgrounds.

Webster's Unabridged Dictionary defines the word "remarkable" as "(1) notably or conspicuously unusual; extraordinary. (2) Worthy of notice or attention." As the reader will come to discover, the women who live on these pages easily meet this criterion. Belle Boyd was just a teenager when she made her mark on history. In contrast, Grandma Gatewood was a woman in her seventies when she epitomized the American mantra, "never give up." Theodate Pope was a child of the

American aristocracy while Bessie Coleman was born a sharecropper's daughter. Elizabeth Black sacrificed her promising career while Laura Keene damaged hers in her failed attempt to artificially inflate it. The Native-American Lady of Cofitechque bravely stood her ground against Spanish conquistadores while the equally courageous Mary Katherine Goddard faced the danger of British wrath and the threat of execution. Marie Tharp's discoveries were made from the confines of her office while Susan Butcher is best described as the consummate outdoor adventurer. Sybil Ludington's name and daring deed faded into obscurity while Grace Hopper went on to become a favorite guest on The Tonight Show with Johnny Carson.

What are the common traits that make up the characters of these extraordinary women? All were fiercely independent. All were courageous and resilient. They were highly intelligent, feisty, self-confident and focused on achieving their individual goals. Some possessed charming personalities while others were demanding and irritating, but all were eager to explore new ideas and opportunities. In other words, these women had grit – the determination to persist and persevere no matter how many or how difficult the obstacles. Some went on to live happy lives and others lived lives of disappointment or obscurity, but all left their mark. The achievements of these amazing women are impressive, important and exceptional.

Let me briefly introduce them to you:

Marie Tharp – Her imagination and imagery led to the revelation of the hidden, largest geological feature on Earth to the scientific community and the public.

Grace Hopper – Rear Admiral of the United States Navy, brilliant mathematician and designer of the COBOL computer language.

Laura Keene – Famous nineteenth century actress who was an eyewitness to the assassination of President Abraham Lincoln.

Theodate Pope – Innovative architect whose trailblazing career opened the door for women to a previously unavailable profession.

Sybil Ludington – Teenager whose midnight ride rivals that of Paul Revere's in daring and importance.

Mary Katherine Goddard – Courageous publisher who defied the British by being the first to print and publish the Declaration of Independence with the names of all its signatories.

Belle Boyd – Combination of unorthodox behavior, unbridled courage and unassailable loyalty to her southern roots led to a career in espionage.

Elizabeth Black – Portrait artist whose gift to World War II GI's and their families was and remains, unique and irreplaceable.

Bessie Coleman – Pioneer aviator and barnstormer who defied bigotry and sexism in her quest to "amount to something."

The Lady of Cofitacheque_– Native-American tribal queen who provided needed and requested assistance to Spanish explorer Hernando DeSoto and was subsequently double-crossed and forced into captivity.

Susan Butcher_– Determined and focused athlete whose name, for many, is synonymous with the "toughest race in the world."

Emma Gatewood – Intrepid elderly woman whose walk in the woods gave rise to a movement that motivated thousands more to follow in her canvas clad footprints.

All the narratives are based on facts. Direct quotations, either spoken or written, are italicized. Other dialogue is a product of my imagination but is in keeping with my study of the character and personality of each woman. A bibliography is included for those who would like to delve further into these extraordinary lives.

Honore de Balzac defined woman as: "A creature between man and the angels." Listen to the voices of these twelve remarkable women. They are not, by any stretch of the imagination, saintly or heavenly beings, but you will find yourself inspired by their stories.

When someone shows you who they really are, believe them.

Maya Angelou

SCIENCE AND THE ARTS

MARIE THARP

My name is Marie Tharp. I was born in Ypsilanti, Michigan during the summer of 1920. My father introduced me to the challenging and fascinating world of maps when I was just a small girl. Papa was a soil surveyor working for the U.S. Department of Agriculture's Bureau of Soils and it seemed as if maps were part of Papa's lifeline. Sometimes, to my great delight, he would take me on the job with him. I felt grown up and privileged to carry his pads and pens and stood by entranced as I watched him draw his map

Papa's job meant that we were continually moving from one area of the country to another. We would move from north to south and then back north again as the weather dictated, living in northern states in the summer and southern states in the winter. *"Usually I was the new kid on the block, the stranger that no one had anything to do with. By the time I developed friends, we'd move on."* I was an only child and the closeness of my family was very important to me.

My parents, William and Bertha, were absolutely devoted to me but did not believe children should be overprotected but left free to explore the world on their own. Every four years we went to Washington, D.C. so Papa could have access to the Soil Bureau's main office and oversee the printing of the surveying maps on which he had been working. One day, when I was about six years old, Mother and I visited the United States Capitol building. I became so excited I left Mother behind and ran up the Capitol's marble steps all the way to the building's dome. My unworried mother sat down on a bench and calmly waited for me to return. She wanted me to have the opportunity, on my own, to survey Washington, D.C. from that high vantage point. There, stretched out before me, was a spectacular view of the Mall and its buildings, monuments and reflecting pool. Eventually, I was brought back to her side by a guard who was not at all happy to find me in a place where I was not supposed to be.

By the time I graduated from high school, I had attended two dozen different schools in about sixteen different cities and states. The first time I saw the ocean was in 1925 when we moved to Pascagoula, Mississippi. It was the first time I had ever seen or felt sand and I fondly recall the cool sensation of its wet ooziness squishing between my toes as Mother and I walked along the shoreline. But it was the sea which made the biggest impact on me. It was like nothing I had ever seen before. Mother explained about the tides and the pull of the moon. I was transfixed. Unfortunately, a few months later, it was time to move north once more. It would be over twenty years before I was to see the ocean again.

In 1926, while I was in first grade, a German geophysicist and meteorologist named Alfred Lothar Wegener advanced a new idea which he called the Continental Drift Theory. He theorized that the earth's surface was constructed from continental plates that moved laterally. Not only that, but he hypothesized that at one point, Earth had all been part of a single land mass called Pangaea, a supercontinent that had been breaking apart and wandering across the surface of Earth for billions of years. While looking at a world map, he pointed out that the continents fit together like a jigsaw puzzle; the east coast of South America fits precisely with the west coast of Africa and the projecting parts of Europe and Africa fit the recesses of the Americas. He believed that the continents drift, break apart and converge and that over billions of years, where they broke away, cracks, rifts and trenches remained and where they collided, ranges of folded mountains appeared. He noted that there were similarities of species and fossils on both sides of the Atlantic as well as similarity of geologic record. He claimed that these facts offered proof that Earth's surface was made up of plates that moved. Wegener's theory of continental drift was ridiculed and disparaged by the entire scientific community. Of course, as I was only six years old at the time, none of this had any meaning for me.

When I was fourteen years old tragedy struck my family. Mother became very ill and died a year later. I don't remember much of that sad time. I guess I just went on automatic pilot, living one day at a time until 1939 when I entered Ohio University as an art major. That did not suit me and I switched to a major in music, specifically the violin, and then I tried German, followed by paleo botany, philosophy, English and finally education. It had always been assumed that I would go to college and become a teacher. *"They didn't specify I had to do that, but it was assumed I couldn't be a soil surveyor like Papa because I was a girl, as much as I loved his work, maps, outdoors, in the field with him."* My career options were the same as they were for all girls – teacher, nurse, librarian, secretary or bookkeeper.

College life for girls was strictly circumscribed. We had to wear heels and hose to dinner. Skirts were required to be full or straight, with hems fifteen and one half inches from the floor. We wore saddle shoes, anklets and high-necked sweaters with pearls. Our hair was cut in a short style with neat, curled bangs. *"Oh God, it was terrible."* I floundered from one major to another, until at last, I discovered geology, a science I found fascinating.

I graduated from Ohio University where I received a Bachelor's degree in geology. However, I had a problem. Geologists were almost always men and it was unlikely that as a woman, I would be allowed to do field work. My mentor at the university suggested I learn drafting, a skill which was not unusual for a geologist and I followed his excellent advice and learned the skill. During my senior year, the University of Michigan offered an accelerated geology Master's degree with a guarantee of a job in the petroleum industry upon graduation. The year was 1942 and most of the men were off fighting in World War II, which meant most of the students were women. We were called the "PG girls," PG being short for petroleum geology. I liked the other women in class, but didn't become close to any of them. As before, I *"lived alone, walked alone, ate alone."*

Not much had changed in the twenty years since the American Association of Petroleum Geologists had publicly derided Wegener's theory of continental drift. There was still no definitive theory that explained how the Earth's crust was formed. Explanations of how mountains, oceans, continents, islands and valleys came into being was still a source of contention. Textbooks were inconclusive and lectures raised more questions than answers.

After graduation, as promised, I was hired by the Standard Oil Company in Tulsa as an assistant to a senior geologist. My job was to help the "real" geologists decide where to drill and when to stop drilling. In order to make these decisions, it was imperative to measure the ocean depths, something man had been trying to determine for hundreds of years. The process of measuring ocean depths is called sounding. In 1523, Ferdinand Magellan is said to have conducted the first single-spot sounding when he lowered a weighted line into the Pacific Ocean. When it reached seven hundred and fifty meters, he declared the ocean "immeasurable." In 1854, a navy man named John Mercer Brooke tied a cannonball to the end of a length of strong rope on which fathoms had been marked off. He threw the cannonball over the side of the boat and waited for it to hit bottom. When it did, a hollow, brass rod shot out capturing sediment. When the rod was raised to the surface, the sediment could be examined under a microscope. It was thought that the ocean floor was flat, a smooth basin that swooped from continent to continent, with sediment slowly filling at the edges until enough was collected at the bottom to emerge from the seawater. In 1856, Matthew Fontaine Maury used this device to make a contour map of the Atlantic Ocean floor with lines drawn in at one, two, three and four thousand fathoms. His map was the first to hint that there was a ridge running down the length of the Atlantic Ocean.

The study of the ocean floor moved ahead excruciatingly slowly. The 1901 formation of the International Hydrographic Bureau headed by Prince Albert I of Monaco gave a certain status to the study of oceanography. By the time World War I broke out in 1914, rudimentary echo sounders had been developed into what is now called sonar. Sonar works by sending out a ping and then measuring the amount of time, after bouncing off the ocean floor, the ping takes to reach a receiver. The urgency to study and locate underwater masses was intensified by the tragic collision of the ocean liner *Titanic* with an underwater iceberg.

I was frustrated by my lowly position at Standard Oil and was "*bored as hell.*" I was limited to filing and pulling maps of the areas where drilling decisions were being made by the male geologists. I found the work I was doing to be tedious. I had a graduate degree in geology "for Pete's sake" and I wanted to do meaningful work like the men were doing. Finally, even though I was earning a very healthy salary of two hundred dollars a month, I had had enough. I quit and enrolled at the University of Tulsa where I received a degree in math. Armed with my excellent credentials, in 1948 I left for New York in search of a job that was interesting and commensurate with my education.

I applied for a job at Columbia University. The secretary told me in no uncertain terms that,"*We ain't got no room for file clerks.*" She quite understandably assumed that as a woman, what other job could I possibly do. I was hired by the department head, Dr. Maurice "Doc" Ewing as an assistant to the male geology graduate students. Sometimes I was told to draft copies of simple maps. However, most of my work was "*strictly arithmetic. I set up equations in one column. Column one plus column two equals column three, then column three times five equals column four, and so on."* In other words, despite my degrees, my function was to be a human calculator assistant to the students.

Doc believed that trying to understand Earth while studying only the thirty per cent of it that was dry was "*like trying to describe a football after being given a look at a piece of lacing.*" However, there were many problems that had to be faced. Commercially available geophysical instruments did not exist. Actually, geophysics as a science did not exist and most oceanographers were interested only in water and the life it contained. Very few thought that exploring the land beneath the sea was worth investigating.

The atmosphere in the lab at Columbia was intellectually stimulating – for the men. They discussed scientific problems, programs and recent discoveries over lunch. I was never invited to join them. Then Doc hired a young geology graduate student named Bruce Heezen and both our lives were to take a decided turnabout. Bruce spent most of his time at sea. When he returned, he could go to the lab and discuss with the others what he had learned about the Earth from his ocean explorations. I could never go to sea. Women were not allowed aboard research vessels. My job was to serve as Bruce's assistant and take his raw data and crunch the numbers. I was kept very busy drafting and plotting the ocean floor profiles using his data.

Our lab was confined to a very small space at Columbia until we were relocated to a one hundred and twenty-five acre estate across the Hudson River. The estate was donated by Florence Lamont, widow of a prominent New York financier. The estate would become home to the

Lamont Geological Observatory. It was wonderful to be able to spread out. I covered the walls of my office with charts representing the world's oceans.

As meticulous as I was in attention to detail regarding my maps and records, I paid very little attention to my wardrobe. I wore what others probably considered bizarre outfits such as an evening gown with sneakers. On more than one occasion I wore a skirt slit up to the knee, a man's shirt and oxfords or tennis shoes. "I didn't go in for the looks of what people were wearing. I look for intelligence."

During World War II, Doc and a colleague had developed a new echo sounder. With this instrument, depth measurements could be recorded nonstop. A sound signal would be sent out at regular intervals, and a microphone inside the hull of the ship would pick up the echo. As a ping was sent out, a stylus would be set in motion downward across a continuously spooled strip of four-inch-wide paper. When the echo returned, the stylus would mark the recording paper by burning it with an electric spark. The instrument worked almost continuously. I say almost continuously, because there was just one small problem. The sounder depended upon the ship's electric power which turned off whenever the door of the ship's refrigerator was opened. Uh-oh!

Bruce and I established a working relationship. I worked exclusively for him and we eventually became a team. Bruce went to sea and collected the data. I processed it. At last I was able to do work that had the potential to advance the study of Earth as well as my own career. The research vessel that Bruce sailed on was named the Atlantis and I kept detailed records of each voyage. Between 1947 and 1952, the Atlantis sailed between the eastern coasts of the Americas and the western coasts of Europe and Africa. Paths, called tracks, were followed during each trip and marked on nautical charts. Latitude and longitude were periodically marked so depths could be matched by location. Armed with this information, we began to work on drawing a map of the ocean floor.

The research ships rarely traveled all the way across the Atlantic. A voyage might begin at Martha's Vineyard and sail just one quarter of the ocean doing experiments, measuring temperature, salinity and seismic refractions, and then return. Another might sail straight to Gibraltar before taking soundings. A third vessel might sail just to the middle of the ocean collecting data. My job was to collect all the data and translate three thousand records into one drawing. This had never been done before. I glued together several strips of linen paper and drew six wide graphs on the sheets. I marked one, two, three and four thousand fathoms on the vertical axis and marked distance in five hundred mile increments along the horizontal axis. My graph resembled a musical staff. I made dots marking the depths and then connected the dots like notes on a musical score with some notes missing. I then inked in below the jagged lines, the six transatlantic topographical profiles. When done, I had the silhouettes of the ocean floor terrains. I observed that there was a wide bump where the ocean floor gained elevation. The bump was on all six profiles which meant a range, not one isolated mountain. "I noticed that in each profile there was a deep notch near the crest of the ridge." The surprising discovery of the rift was new information.

I was very excited and immediately called Bruce. When I showed him my work he groaned and said, "It cannot be. It looks too much like continental drift." His comment resulted in our first fight. Our fights were later to become legendary but at the time, it was shocking. We each were adamant about our respective positions. There was a lot of finger jabbing and shouting. In subsequent fights, we would argue about what went where and what to do when there was no data. In my fury, I may have thrown a paperweight or two at his head. It was not unknown for him to retaliate by erasing weeks of my work with an electric eraser. We were both simultaneously infuriated and nervous. You see, as geologists, we each realized that my discovery of the existence of the rift meant that Wegener's theory of continental drift was substantiated. This was nothing short of geological heresy. Bruce was horrified and refused to believe it. Prior to my drafting the map, no one else had seen the big picture of the Mid-Atlantic Ridge system.

Bruce dismissed my map assumptions as "girl talk." However, it was always his philosophy "to go from the known to the unknown." With his blessing, I started again with a huge sheet of blank paper and began plotting firstly the well-known information. I began with a latitude and longitude grid. Then I traced in the borders of the continents. I penciled in the ships' tracks. I sketched out the terrain of the ocean floor around the coastlines of the Americas, Europe, and northern Africa. In many areas there was no data but I kept on going. I extrapolated that in areas where there were no soundings, there was a rift valley. Bruce and I found a definite association of topography with seismicity meaning that earthquake epicenters clustered in the rift valley. I plotted, drew, checked, corrected, redrew and rechecked.

Six months later, I was able to sketch one nearly continuous rift valley all across the world. It was a forty-thousand-mile-long underwater structure which quite possibly was the largest geologic feature on Earth. It stretches from the northern Atlantic Ocean south all the way around the tip of Africa east into the Indian Ocean. It then continues to the southern Pacific Ocean and then turns north again to the northern Pacific Ocean off the western coast of North America reaching almost to Alaska. To put the discovery of the forty-thousand mile-long ridge in perspective, the circumference of the earth at the equator is twenty-four thousand, nine hundred and one miles. *"Establishing the rift valley and the mid-ocean ridge that went all the way around the world for 40,000 miles – that was something important. You could only do that once. You can't find anything bigger than that, at least on this planet."*

Bruce hired a Fine Arts student to plot underwater earthquake epicenters to get a better sense of the ocean's currents. The student's map was made to the identical scale of my map. When the art student's earthquake map was overlaid on top of my map on a light table, the result was incredible - the earthquakes lined up "like buttons on a flute" along the Mid-Atlantic Ridge. The meaning was clear to me; continental drift was real. It took another two years, but by 1953, Bruce finally accepted the idea.

In 1956, Bruce announced our findings at a meeting of the American Geophysical Union in Toronto, The reaction in the scientific community ranged from amazement, to skepticism, to scorn. Jacques Cousteau, the famed oceanographer, did not at first believe in the rift valley and he set out to prove us wrong. In order to confirm our mistake, he towed a movie camera on a sled behind his boat, the *Calypso*, and dragged the camera along the ocean floor. To his surprise, he found our rift valley and showed his movie at the first International Ocean Congress in New York in 1959. "He took beautiful movies of big black cliffs in blue water." The confirmation of our findings by the celebrated oceanographer helped convince many scientific skeptics to at last accept the existence of the rift valley. Although our map was a joint effort and had both our names on it, I was never invited to present a paper or speak at any geologic conference despite the fact that I was one of the few, either man or woman, oceanographic cartographers in the world. Strangely, I did not really mind that much that Bruce got all the glory. "I felt lucky to have a job that was so interesting."

By now, Bruce's life and mine were completely intertwined. I had started out as his assistant and then we became a team. We were always together except when Bruce was at sea. We worked together, ate together, argued together and traveled together. In 1962, I bought a large Dutch colonial house overlooking the Hudson River in Nyack, New York. In 1962, it was uncommon for a single woman to buy a house, especially such a stately home. Bruce was a very frequent visitor. He would come to my house for dinner and often stayed over. The others in our workplace thought of us as a couple and we thought of ourselves as a couple. Whether or not we also were lovers is our business.

In 1967, National Geographic Magazine published our map of the Indian Ocean painted by Austrian artist, Heinrich Bergann. The Magazine's supplemental map was the kind that people pulled out and saved even after the issue itself had been discarded. At the time, National

Geographic Magazine had six million subscribers. Both Bruce and I were delighted as we wanted to help people see images of things that distance, access and cost prevented them from seeing in person. The ocean floor was one of those things.

We both believed that the oceans were part of one interconnected system. We recognized five distinct oceans – the Atlantic, Pacific, Indian, Arctic and the area around Antarctica. In 1973, along with artist Heinrich Bergann, we were commissioned by the Office of Naval Research to paint a panorama map of the entire world's ocean floor. Our map would show, for the first time, what was under the seventy percent of the Earth's surface that was hidden by water.

Bruce had the proofs of the panorama with him on board the research submarine *NR-1* when he had a heart attack and died. The date was June 21, 1977. He was 53 years old. We had been together for eighteen years. We did not have children – we had maps. I felt "as if my life had just been cut in two." Although we had never married, I thought of myself as his widow and others treated me as if I were his widow. I chose what others might characterize as an unconventional way of coping with his death. As mentioned earlier, I never was interested in being a "fashionista" so I took to wearing Bruce's clothing. I hired a local seamstress to cut Bruce's pants and piece them together to make gored skirts for me. I wore his button-down shirts and attempted to make them more feminine by adding embroidery flourishes.

Our World Ocean Floor Panorama Map was, at last, printed on May 17, 1978. I thought it "beautiful with perfect registration and gorgeous colors." It showed the Mid-Atlantic ridge snaking across the Earth. A rift valley ran down the center of the entire ridge, the feature that I had discovered twenty-six years before. The map was colored in purplish red, ochre and deep grayish blue for the ocean floor. Ochre landmasses slowly evolved into orange mountains. Fissures and trenches were blue/black. The oceans, carefully defined, washed gracefully in around continents and countries. How I wished Bruce were alive to see it.

I dealt with Bruce's death by keeping busy and spent the next thirty years of my life trying to complete everything that he had been working on before he died. I spent most of my time and money on what I called the Bruce Project. His legacy was what was important to me. I arranged for Bruce's papers, letters, logs, books, films he took on submersibles, slides and maps to be accepted by the Smithsonian Institution and transferred to its Archives. I traveled to Washington, D.C. to oversee the transfer wearing one of my "imaginative" outfits. The Iranian hostage situation was in full bloom at the time. To the embarrassment of everyone, I was mistaken for a terrorist and frisked.

As the years passed, health issues cropped up and when I was in my seventies, I needed to be hospitalized. One night I became hungry at an off-hour. The nurse told me that meals were served on a regular schedule and I would have to wait. She couldn't possibly be serious. I was hungry now. I got dressed, unhooked myself from the various monitoring devices and walked across the street where I had a meal at a diner. After I ate, I walked back to the hospital, put my hospital gown back on and got into bed. Nothing to it! Turns out, the hospital staff had "freaked out" when they realized I was missing.

1997 was a banner year for me as I was the recipient of two honors from the Library of Congress. The first honor was from the Geography and Map Division's Philip Lee Phillips Society, a national organization formed to help further the public's understanding of cartography. I was named by them as one of the four greatest cartographers of the twentieth century.

That year was also the one hundredth anniversary of the Library of Congress' Jefferson Building. To commemorate the occasion, The Library put on an exhibition titled American Treasures from the Library of Congress. I was invited to attend the opening night gala along with many other dignitaries including President Bill Clinton. Everyone pretty much ignored the old woman wearing a colorfully "fanciful" outfit riding about in a wheelchair. We all were awestruck by what we were seeing. On exhibit were the contents of Abraham Lincoln's pockets the night he was assassinated, maps drawn by George Washington when he was a surveyor, a rough draft of the Declaration of Independence and pages from the journals of Lewis and Clark. And then, there it was, taking its place among the other Treasures – one of my maps of the ocean floor. When I saw it, I started to cry. I couldn't have been more proud and honored!

EPILOGUE

Marie Tharp died of advanced lung cancer in August, 2006. Her work was the "start of seeing our planet in a whole new way." The first copy of the World Ocean Floor Panorama, conceptualized by Bruce Heezen and Marie Tharp, painted by Heinrich Bergann, funded by the U.S.

Department of Naval Research, rolled off the presses on May 7, 1978. Despite all the new technologies, even at this point, only ten per cent of the ocean floor had been surveyed and studied in any detail. Scientists have mapped Venus and Mars in more detail than Earth.

Also during this year, Marie Tharp and Bruce Heezen were awarded the Hubbard Medal from the National Geographic Society, its highest award. It had only been awarded thirty-four times since 1906. Other recipients include Roald Amundsen, Sir Earnest Shackleton and Richard Byrd.

The recognition, or lack thereof of Marie's work, was profoundly affected by her gender. She was not permitted to go on research vessels' expeditions, but was forced to collect information about the ocean floor by forming a partnership with Bruce Heezen who could go on ships. All her work had to carry Bruce's name for it to be accepted. She was never invited to present their work at conferences or lectures; it was always Bruce who served as their spokesperson. To her credit, she never became bitter about this unfair arrangement. While it is true she wanted credit to be given where credit was due, she focused on getting the information out and available for people to see, touch and read. The love of her work always outweighed her desire to be recognized.

Until the publication of Marie Tharp and Bruce Heezen's work, more had been known about the structure of stars than about the oceans probably because stars are visible and the ocean floor is covered. To make the public believe that the invisible land covered by water is a reality, the world needed to see their data illustrated by their beautiful and detailed maps. When their maps were published, they contributed to a revolution in geological thinking. *"Scientists and the general public got their first relatively realistic maps of a vast part of the planet they could never see."*

The Heezen-Tharp Collection containing forty thousand pieces, ninety thousand square feet of maps, atlases and globes has been housed in the Library of Congress' Madison Building basement in its Geography and Map Division since 1995. In 2001, Marie Tharp was awarded the First Lamont Heritage Award. The Russian version of the novel *The Hunt for Red October* has one of her maps printed on its endpapers.

NOTES ON BRUCE HEEZEN

Bruce Heezen was born in Vinton, Iowa on April 11, 1924. His college career was interrupted by World War II. During this period, farmworkers were in short supply. Bruce hoped that if he were working on a farm when his draft number came up he would be given an exemption. His work on a turkey farm led him to vow he would never be a farmer. He was to hate turkey his whole life. When his draft number came up, he was classified 4-F when doctors discovered he had high blood pressure. He earned his undergraduate degree from the University of Iowa; his Masters and PhD degrees were both from Columbia University.

Bruce was a man who liked to be in charge. He made intimidation the dominating characteristic of his public and work personna. In private he was generous and friendly. "Colorful" language was evident in his everyday discourse both on and off the job. He enjoyed food. He turned the *NR-1* submarine into a "nuclear powered delicatessen with strings of preserved sausages, sweetbreads, canned delicacies and jars of treats that he stuffed into any crevasse he could find and hung them from overhead cables." An oceanographic survey ship was christened USNS Bruce Heezen in his honor in 1999.

"The sea, our sea, thou great and glorious sea

Yield up thy secrets to our weak and fumbling band

Honors, titles and epithets are but empty words for joy of teaching, joy of learning

Joy at the instants of revelation are our life's real rewards."

Bruce Heezen

GRACE HOPPER

"Ladies and Gentlemen, it is my great honor to introduce Admiral Grace Hopper."

Upon hearing these words, I rise from my seat on the stage and accompanied by enthusiastic applause, step up to the podium. Frequently invited to speak at conferences and meetings of scientists, mathematicians and military personnel, I have learned to feel very comfortable in this type of circumstance. My name is Grace Murray Hopper and I can proudly say that I have earned the rank of Rear Admiral of the United States Navy, one of very few women to do so.

Being in a predominately male environment is nothing new for me. My entire career has been in the world of men and I am completely at ease and enjoy their company. Even as a child, I was fascinated by so-called "boy's" toys and interests. Understanding how things worked sparked my curiosity and my parents readily encouraged my brother, sister and me to experiment and ask questions. When I was about seven years old I wanted to understand how an alarm clock worked. I completely dismantled seven household clocks before my mother discovered what I was doing. She quite reasonably insisted that in the future I limit my destruction of the family timepieces to one single clock.

I graduated Phi Beta Kappa from Vassar College in 1928 with a Bachelor's degree in mathematics and physics, followed by a Master's degree from Yale University which, in turn, was followed in 1934, by a Ph.D. in mathematics also from Yale. While studying at Yale, I returned to Vassar to teach mathematics and in 1930, married New York University professor Vincent Foster Hopper. The marriage lasted fifteen years and I kept his surname.

World War II interrupted my career at Vassar and in 1943 I took a leave of absence from my professorial duties and was sworn into the United States Naval Reserve. I wanted to follow my grandfather's footsteps and join the Navy but women were not permitted in the Navy back then. We had our own volunteer unit called the WAVES (Women Accepted for Voluntary Emergency Service). They had to give me a special exemption to enlist as I was fifteen pounds under the Navy's minimum weight of one hundred twenty pounds. The establishment of the WAVES did not sit well with some of the older Admirals and it was said by some that, *"if the Navy could possibly have used dogs or ducks or monkeys…it probably would have preferred them to women."*

I graduated first in my class and was assigned to the Bureau of Ordinance Computation Project at Harvard University as a Lieutenant, junior grade. I was the third person to join the research team headed by professor and Naval Reserve Lieutenant, Howard H. Aiken. He greeted me with the words, *"Where the hell have you been? I can't believe they sent me a woman."* Pointing to his electromechanical computer machine called the Mark 1, he barked, *"Here, complete the coefficients of the arc tangent series by next Thursday."* With those words, my life changed.

There is nothing I enjoy more than a good challenge so I took a deep breath and plunged right in. Aiken handed me a thin code book and gave me one week to learn how to program "the beast" (as he fondly labeled the Mark 1) and to get a program running. Well, as I said, I relish a challenge and in short order, I learned how to program the Mark 1.

There was no precedent for what we were doing at Harvard. Everything on the Mark 1 was being done for the first time. I had been working at the Lab for under a year when one day Aiken walked up to my desk and told me I was going to write a book. I tried protesting that I had never written a book. He dismissed my objection with a curt, *"Well, you're in the Navy now."* I ended up writing a five hundred and sixty-one page manual that gave a full and detailed description of the Mark 1. My manual described all of its parts and circuits, and contained samples of all kinds of programming. Every day, I would write about five pages and read them aloud to Aiken. If he didn't like what I wrote, I had to do it over. The book was titled "*Manual for the Automatic Sequence-Controlled Calculator.*" In the book, I described my design for a new kind of timing chart with circuit diagrams corresponding to it that showed the sequence of operations. Back in those days you really had to know every relay and how it was working or you couldn't debug a program.

The Mark 1 had very little resemblance to the computers of today. It was fifty feet long, eight feet tall, and eight feet deep, filling an entire room. It had more than seven hundred and fifty thousand parts, five hundred and thirty miles of wire and three million wire connections. Its four horsepower motor and a drive shaft drove all the mechanical parts by a system of interlocking gears, switches and control circuits. A particular idiosyncrasy was that it would stop dead at an end of an operation unless the number seven or some other signal had been entered to tell it to go on to the next operation.

Because of the war, we worked under enormous pressure. The Mark 1 calculations were essential to the rapid new developments in technology and weaponry such as advances in aircraft, missiles, guided missiles and depth charges. It seemed that everyone who submitted problems to the Lab demanded immediate answers. We received several requests for calculations from John von Neumann of the Los Alamos National Laboratory in New Mexico. He was working on problems dealing with spherical shock waves based on atomic fission and the difficult implosion problems for detonating plutonium.

Early programming was extremely basic. The programmer had to tell the computer what to do in minute steps broken down into addition or subtraction and then put it in a sequence. The instructions were then put on a manual tape punch, the tape was put in the computer and then with fingers crossed, the programmer hoped the program would run. The process was tedious and frustratingly slow involving many, many hours, if not days, of repetitive work. However, the atmosphere in the Lab was frenzied, exciting and yes, fun. The backwards running clock I had hung on my office wall was a source of much amusement for my co-workers.

When the war ended, Vassar offered me a full professorship but I turned it down. I simply liked computers better. I was in on the beginning of something new. A whole new field was opening and I wanted to be part of the new imaginative visions and excitement. I thought I could make a valuable contribution. Promoted to Lieutenant in 1944, I tried to transfer to the regular Navy as they were now accepting women. Alas, at age thirty-eight, I was two years past the cutoff age and had to stay in the Naval Reserves. I joined the Eckhart-Mauchley Computer Corporation in Philadelphia, (later taken over by Remington Rand) operators of the UNIVAC 1. I focused on methods to speed up the writing of coding instructions that ran individual programs. At that time, there was much rivalry between “hardware” and “software” proponents, each group blaming the other for errors and glitches. I wasn’t much interested in hardware or as I liked to say, *“the part of the computer that you can kick.”*

The UNIVAC 1 was the first commercial large-scale electronic computer. It was fourteen and a half feet long, seven and a half feet wide, and eight feet high, still enormous by today’s standards, but much smaller than the Mark 1. Most importantly, it was over three hundred times faster. While the Mark 1 could complete three operations per second, the UNIVAC 1 could complete one thousand operations per second. (In comparison, by 1963 the CD66600 could execute three million instructions per second. In 2008, an IBM supercomputer processed 1.026 quadrillion calculations per second.) The UNIVAC 1 was an alpha-numeric device that was capable of handling letters as well as numbers. It could accommodate all the characters of a standard keyboard typewriter and used magnetic tape to receive data instead of the old punch tape.

Programming remained prohibitively slow as it still involved writing minute instructions for each calculation. Hardware was developing at such a rapid pace that the software simply could not keep up. Programming had become a bottleneck. I realized that there must be a better way and hit upon the idea of a compiler. A compiler would turn worded instructions into code that could be read by computers. Up to now, computer calculations were dependent on a programmer writing the same set of instructions for the computer to follow even when the calculations had different objectives. Pages and pages of duplicate code had to be written which was tedious, time-consuming and prone to errors. To eliminate the need for the programmer to write the code, I designed, developed and implemented a three-letter call sign that when programmed, would allow the computer to retrieve instructions from its own library. What had previously taken months of programming time, the computer could now accomplish in five minutes.

It seemed to me, that in the future, users would be interested in how quickly data would flow between input and output and only professional programmers would need to understand the code representing operations. I believed that the computer itself could do the work now being done by the programmer. I was met with lots of opposition. Not surprising because I have long observed that, *"Humans are allergic to change. They love to say, we've always done it this way. I try to fight that. That's why I have that clock on my wall that runs counter-clockwise."* Many in the field argued that computers could only do arithmetic and obviously could not write programs. Well, a little opposition never stops me and I insisted that in the future, compiling routines of all sorts would be devised, and further, that I could make a computer do anything I could completely define. I predicted that in the future, computers would be able to handle commercial programs as well as mathematical programs. With the construction of a compiler, the programmer would be free from spending inordinate amounts of time writing code and may return to being a mathematician. Programs could be written and debugged in hours instead of weeks and the results would be accurate.

Slowly, the number of computers began growing and expanding into the private sectors as banks, insurance companies and others began using computers for inventories and payrolls. To the astonishment of nearly everyone, the UNIVAC 1, bought by the A.C. Neilsen Company, with only seven per cent of the votes counted, correctly predicted the landslide victory of the 1952 presidential election of Dwight David Eisenhower over Adlai Stevenson.

I realized that it was imperative that if computers were going to become a widespread saleable item, it would be necessary to make them easier to program and also capable of communicating with each other. Somehow, people-oriented data must become translatable into machine code. At the time, high-level programming language was non-existent. There was only machine code; each code completely different as they were written for different machines. I began working on an English language compiler whereby the computer would translate letters of the alphabet into machine code that could be read by computers. This idea was not mine but was originated by Alan Turing, the British mathematician. I proposed creating a plain English compiler which would be of prime use for businesses. The idea was to make computers accessible to as many people as possible. No one supported this idea and I could not get funding. In my usual bull-headed fashion, I went ahead with the idea on my own. I believe that *"when you have a good idea and you've tried it and you know it's going to work, go ahead and do it – because it's much easier to apologize afterwards than it is to get permission."* In 1960, I, along with several colleagues, introduced the first version of COBOL, (Common Business Oriented Language). The Navy and other organizations quickly accepted the high level language as it was capable of running on different machines produced by different manufacturers. COBOL soon became the ubiquitous language for business and it and other high level languages such as FORTRAN (Formula Translation) became defined and standardized throughout the data processing community.

I was happy for my hard-fought success in the world of computers but found that I missed the early days of computing when everyone was excited and the atmosphere was alive with possibilities. Then, no one knew what could or could not be done and anything could happen. Now, the industry had begun to settle down and I missed the adrenalin rush of new discoveries regarding the machines. Competition between the Remington Rand Company and IBM (International Business Machines) was intense. I realized that salesmanship was critical. I didn't have much in the way of praise for IBM and thought the company to be shortsighted and secretive. I still loved the Navy and remained in the Navy Reserves. Throughout my civilian career, it was the Navy which had given me the most support and it was the Navy which led the way in innovative computer usage.

While I was still working for Remington Rand, the Navy requested that I be allowed to give a series of talks on digital computers to reserve officers. Despite the huge impact that computers had made in military and commercial fields, there still was much resistance to the new technology. At the risk of sounding like a braggart, I knew how to be an effective speaker (remember, I was a former professor) and could explain how to bridge the gap between civilian and military use of the new technology. I was able to speak about computers and programming in both technical and non-technical terms, depending on the composition of the audience. Thanks in no small part to Dr. Aiken at the Harvard Computation Lab and his insistence that I write the manual for the Mark 1, I had also mastered the art of writing with clarity no matter how complicated the subject. As it turned out, I would continue speaking for the Navy for the next thirty-three years. In 1957, I was promoted to the rank of Commander and was duly recognized as an expert in electronic computer design and programming.

Blessed with an inordinate amount of energy, I kept myself very busy. In addition to my day job at Remington Rand, I continued working as a naval reservist at night and on weekends. I also taught classes in business and industrial applications of computers in evening classes. My Navy superiors thought I should be promoted to Captain but only one woman at a time could be authorized to hold that rank and it was filled.

In 1966, I received a letter from the Chief of Naval Personnel. The letter stated that I had served for twenty-three years which was more than twenty. I knew that. It also said that I was about to turn sixty. I knew that too. The final paragraph asked me to apply for retirement which I reluctantly did, effective December 31, 1966. It was the saddest day of my life.

Hold on! Seven months after retiring, the Navy recalled me to active duty for a special assignment in Washington. It amuses me to point out that I was in the reserve, retired, and on active duty all at the same time. My assignment was to standardize computer languages for all Navy computers not part of weapons systems. The problem was that there were many incompatible versions of COBOL as each hardware vendor chose features, made their own "innovative" features, and removed those features they didn't like. So a COBOL program written for a UNIVAC computer would not run on an IBM or RCA computer. It became my job to fix the problem. Oh yes, and by the way, in August of 1973, six years after returning to active duty, I finally was promoted to Captain. It took an act of Congress for me to get that promotion because at the age of sixty-six, I was over-age for a regular upgrade in rank. I suspect that the real reason I got the promotion was because of my frequent speaking engagements, *"the Navy wanted me to have enough ribbons to look impressive."*

I still felt like and had the energy of a young chick. As noted earlier, normal retirement age for the Navy was sixty-two but I spent another nine years lecturing my superiors and everyone else about computer technology. I was often accused of being contrary and cantankerous, (true), but never wrong in my analysis (also true). I must admit I took advantage of my age and gender to cut through much of the nonsense of politics and bureaucracy. At the same time, I kept busy with a strenuous schedule of travel and talks. I gave over two hundred speeches a year that took me all over the world always proudly wearing my Navy uniform. Like any good lecturer, I kept a stable of stories that I could pull out at appropriate times and tried to keep my speeches extemporaneous, informative and entertaining. I was often asked why satellite communications took so long and I explained by using visual aids. I would hand out a piece of wire cut into 11.8 inch lengths to each member of the audience. I told them that each length of wire represented how far electricity could travel in one billionth of a second or one nanosecond. I then would show the audience a coil of wire nearly a thousand feet long. The coil represented a microsecond. It would become obvious to the audience that a coil of wire is a lot shorter than the distance to a satellite.

As time went on, I found that I was spending less time with "hands-on" work with computers and spending more time lecturing about its future. Resistance to change had continually plagued advances in technology and the resistance continued as we moved forward. In my lectures, I talked about standards and office systems. I tried to paint a picture of the future and the part played by computers in everyday living. I envisioned a future time when all our personal data would be on a little card about the size of a drivers' license. I spoke about the importance of inspiring young people to enter the field and for senior workers to listen to them and their ideas.

I was now seventy years old and certainly not ready to stop working. I joined the Digital Equipment Corporation where I represented the company at industry forums speaking on governmental issues. I was still hooked on *"Lucky Strike"* cigarettes. Smoking was beginning to be frowned upon by many companies and was banned in many offices including Digital. I told them, *"You can either put an ashtray in my office or I won't be coming in."* My office was made a designated smoking area. I kept up my strenuous travel schedule flying all over the country speaking at forums and conferences although I was becoming increasingly troubled by falls and broken bones.

In 1983, I was promoted to Commodore in a special ceremony held in the Oval Office hosted by President Ronald Reagan. I wore my Navy uniform, and under my cap, my customary hairnet over my thinning hair. Probably due to my lifetime of chain smoking, my face was deeply lined, but nevertheless, I wore very little make-up. However, as was my habit, my nails were beautifully manicured. I invited my brother, sister, nephews and their families to the ceremony. The President wore a brown suit and cowboy boots. Never shy, I insisted he have his picture taken with my teenaged grandniece, Jennifer. And he did. Actually, he seemed quite amused that I had no reservations at all about ordering him around.

In 1985, the Navy merged the post of Commodore with the rank of Rear Admiral (lower half) and I became just .the sixth woman to achieve that rank. I retired one year later after serving forty-three years in the Navy. The ceremony took place on the one hundred eighty-nine-year-old frigate, *Constitution,* fondly called *"Old Ironsides,"* which was docked in Boston Harbor. I wore my dress whites and gloves and carried my old Navy handbag. The boatswain piped me aboard. In front of two hundred seventy-five relatives, friends and Navy officers, I was presented with the Defense Department's highest award, the Defense Distinguished Service Medal. A Navy band played patriotic songs and I was presented with forty-three roses, one for each year of my naval service. At seventy-nine years, eight months and five days, I was the oldest active duty commissioned officer in the United States Navy. It was quite a day. I called some friends in Philadelphia to request a favor. I asked them to keep an eye on my grandfather Russell's grave. I suspected that, *"the thought of a female admiral might cause him to rise from the dead."*

By 1991, I was approaching 85 and due to severe osteoporosis, rarely left my Arlington, Virginia apartment. That year, President George H.W. Bush awarded me the nation's highest technology award, the National Medal of Technology in a ceremony held in the White House Rose Garden. I chose not to attend the ceremony. I had fallen, broken an ankle and was stuck temporarily in a wheelchair. There was no way I was going to appear in public in that condition. I instructed my sister Mary who received the medal on my behalf to just send it to me in the mail.

EPILOGUE

"Amazing Grace" as her many admirers referred to her, died on January 1, 1992 at the age of eighty-five and was interred in Arlington National Cemetery with full military honors. She is often called the "mother of COBOL." The United States destroyer USS Hopper is named for her as well as the Cray XE6 "Hopper" supercomputer. She was the recipient of innumerable awards and medals as well as thirty-four honorary degrees. When asked about her contributions to technology she replied, *"The most important thing I've accomplished, other than building the compiler, is training young people. They come up to me, you know, and say, Do you think we can do this"? I say, try it. And I back 'em up. They need that. I keep track of them as they get older and I stir 'em up at intervals so they don't forget to take chances."* As for her innumerable honors, she said," *I've received many honors and I'm grateful for them; but I've already received the highest award I'll ever receive, and that has been the privilege and honor of serving proudly in the United States Navy."*

In addition to those awards and medals previously noted, there were many, many others of which the following is just a sample:

1969: Awarded the inaugural Computer Sciences Man of the Year award from the Data Processing Management Association.

1971: The annual Grace Murray Hopper Award for Outstanding Young Computer Professionals was established by the Association for Computing Machinery.

1975: First American and first woman of any nationality to be made a Distinguished Fellow of the British Computer Society.

1986: Received the Defense Distinguished Service Medal.

1988: Received the Golden Gavel Award at the Toastmasters International convention in Washington, D.C.

1991: Received the National Medal of Technology

2001: The Gracies, the Government Technology Leadership Award was named in her honor:

2009: The Department of Energy's National Energy Research Scientific Computing Center named its flagship system, "Hopper."

2016: Awarded the Presidential Medal of Freedom by President Barack Obama.

She was a favorite guest on popular late night television programs such as *The Tonight Show with Johnny Carson* and *The David Letterman Show*. Always dressed in her Navy Admiral uniform, she was informative as well as entertaining. She explained computer technology to the enthralled large television audiences by telling some of her backlog of stories and by using her favorite visual aids – a length of wire 11.8 inches long and a nearly one thousand foot coil of wire.

There are many crowd-pleasing anecdotes told in computer programming circles about the legendary Grace Hopper. Perhaps the most famous describes the time in 1947 when a moth became stuck in a relay resulting in the program not running. Hopper removed the insect and said she was "debugging" the program. Although the story was later deemed to be fallacious, she is credited with popularizing the term, "debugging." In 2013, Google made a Google Doodle in celebration of her one hundred seventh birthday. It is an animation of Hopper sitting at a computer, using COBOL to print out her age. At the end of the animation, a moth flies out of the computer.

LAURA KEENE

I was born in Winchester, England on July 20, 1826 so I suppose one could argue that *technically* I am not an American. However, my highly successful career has taken place in this country, and as it soon will become readily apparent, I played a unique role in one of the most momentous and tragic events in American history.

At birth, I was named Mary Frances Moss. When I was eighteen years old, I married British Army Officer, Henry Wellington Taylor and we had two daughters, Emma and Clara Marie Stella. After his discharge from the army, my husband opened a tavern. Unfortunately, about a year later, he was convicted of a felony, the nature of which I was unaware. As punishment for his crime, he was exiled to Australia on a prison ship, leaving me utterly alone with two small children. My situation was desperate.

My aunt, Elizabeth Yates, was an actress and she advised me to pursue a career on the stage. I believed this to be excellent advice but there was one major drawback. At that time, it was socially unacceptable for a woman with children and no husband to pursue a career in the theater. I overcame this obstacle by giving my children to my widowed mother to raise. To further obfuscate my background, I changed my name to Laura Keene.

I performed on the stage in England for about a year, when American theater owner, James William Wallack, recognizing my talent, offered me the position of leading lady in the stock company of his very successful New York theater. I accepted and not surprisingly, my acting career rapidly blossomed into a triumph. I had earlier divorced Mr. Taylor and during my first season with Wallack's company, I met and married a gambler named John Lutz. John urged me to form my own company which he financed. He also brought my mother and daughters to New York. I was now actress, theater manager and director of my own company, *Laura Keene Varieties*. I was the first woman to assume the role of manager in the up to now all-male managerial arena of New York. I was particularly talented in staging and my reputation for mounting a play was unparalleled. The actors in my company referred to me behind my back as "the Duchess" but I did not mind. I insisted upon absolute professionalism at all costs and enforced strict rules of discipline.

As an actress, I was often considered, and I say this in all modesty, the "first lady of the American theater." Critics referred to me as "an American treasure" an appellation of which I am very proud. I appeared on stages from Boston and New York to Washington D.C. When I am on stage, I am in total command and deservedly receive the utmost respect and admiration from the audience. Leading actors such as renowned and respected John Dyott, young Harry Hawk and John Wilkes Booth have often vied for the opportunity to play opposite me. John Booth's brother, Edwin, and I have appeared on the stage together many times but we rarely get along. On the other hand, I have always liked Harry Hawk. He is twenty-eight years old, short, red-haired and just meant for comedic roles which he plays to great effect. It is said that he is a favorite of President Lincoln. As for John Booth, I find him to be an extremely handsome man and a fairly good actor, well-liked by some but described by others as cold and aloof. Personally, I find him to be rather arrogant and too full of himself, if you know what I mean.

At this point, I would like to describe to you, from my perspective, the events that occurred that fateful night of Friday, April 14, 1865 at Ford's Theater in Washington D.C. As you may recall, I was the headlining star in the delightful farce, *Our American Cousin.* As a matter of fact, that night I was celebrating my one-thousandth performance in the role of Florence Trenchard, a role for which I habitually received critical acclaim. Despite the frequency of playing this role, I always bring something fresh to the part. But, I digress. On this particular night everyone backstage was all a-twitter. There was a rumor that the President and Mrs. Lincoln, with General and Mrs. Grant as their guests, would be attending the performance that night. Poor man! He needed a night out. He has been under such terrible strain dealing with that dreadful war.

When the news of the President's attendance became known to the public, we actors knew we would play before a sold-out house. Tickets were seventy-five cents each and the performance was slated to begin at eight o'clock. At the last minute, the Grants decided to forgo the performance and take the train to Baltimore, the first part of their journey to visit their children in New Jersey. In their stead, the President invited Major Rathbone and his fiancée, Clara Harris.

The President and his party arrived at the theater late, about a half-hour after the eight o'clock opening scene, and were ushered to the President's Box. Mr. Lincoln was seated comfortably in his favorite red horsehair upholstered rocking chair. In the President's honor, the Box railing was elegantly draped with red, white, and blue bunting. After the President and his party were seated, the play was stopped temporarily, the house lights were turned up full and the orchestra played *"Hail to the Chief."* The air was festive and the audience cheered and applauded. The lights were then dimmed and the play resumed. I, naturally, was performing up to my usual legendary standard and the audience was responding in kind, laughing in the appropriate spots and appreciating all the actors' efforts with resounding applause.

The third act began with the audience still laughing delightedly at every humorous line. As the third scene of Act lll began, I was standing in the wings near the prompter's desk waiting for my cue. Harry Hawk, acting the role of Asa Trenchard, was alone on the stage as he delivered his lines, *"Don't know the manners of good society, eh? Well I guess I know enough to turn you inside out, old gal – you sockdologizing old mantrap."* The audience laughed uproariously while simultaneously a loud crack rang out. What was that? Was it a gunshot? The audience began screaming and the entire theater seemed to explode into pandemonium. There were hysterical shouts. Women fainted. Children cried. Confusion was everywhere. No one understood what was happening. Someone cried out that the President had been shot.

Above the fray I heard a voice shout out "*Sic temper tyrannis!*" I saw a man try to hurl himself over the railing of the President's Box but one of his feet became entangled in the bunting and he landed on the stage with a resounding thump. I looked at the man's face and, my stars, it was John Wilkes Booth, and he bellowed in pain. He had broken his leg in the leap from the President's Box. He rose quickly, hobbled across the stage, bumped into me standing in the wings and disappeared into the night. In the theater pandemonium reigned and there were even shouts of, *"Burn the damn place down."* In an effort to compose the frenzied situation, I walked to center stage and cried out for everyone in the theater to remain calm but my words went unheeded.

I looked up at the President's Box and saw Mr. Lincoln slumped over to one side with his head resting on the railing. Mrs. Lincoln was hysterical and kept calling her husband's name. I hastily took a circuitous route through the frenzied throng and up a backstage staircase which led to the Presidential Box.

The Box was filled with theatergoers trying to get a peek at Mr. Lincoln. The fallen President was stretched out on the floor and was being attended to, by among others, young Dr. Charles Leale. I pushed my way past the crowd and knelt down by Mr. Lincoln and tenderly cradled his head in my lap. Blood and confusion and noise were everywhere; the blood from the President's wound staining my yellow silk costume. I felt as if he and I were characters in a traumatically gruesome tableau. Mrs. Lincoln appeared to be in shock and stared at her husband uncomprehendingly.

Dr. Leale recognized that the President needed to be lying on a bed and not the dirty floor. He ordered that Mr. Lincoln be carried across the street to a rooming house. Assuming the commanding position of a Director, I pushed myself to the head of the makeshift procession and we started our solemn journey down the staircase. In my dress stained with the President's blood, I led the way. Dr. Leale followed walking backwards, supporting the President's head. He was followed by two soldiers who carried Mr. Lincoln's upper body while two more soldiers carried his legs. In stunned silence, Mrs. Lincoln brought up the rear of our sorrowful cortege. We slowly descended the stairs and into the chaos of the theatergoers. The audience was running about in a frenzy, yelling and pushing. The actors, too, were in a state of panic as they feared they would be arrested. The noise was overwhelming. I remained at the theater's entrance as the mournful procession continued on without me to the Peterson house across 10th Street.

I never saw President Lincoln alive again.

EPILOGUE

Historians have well-documented the aftermath of that fateful night. Much has been written about John Wilkes Booth and his fellow conspirators. By contrast, very little has been written about the actors whose lives were also irrevocably changed.

Laura Keene was the actor most affected by the events that took place at Ford's theater. She, as well as the other actors in *Our American Cousin,* would forever be associated by the public with the assassination. She would especially be a victim of the unwanted connection because of the publicity attached to her blood-stained dress. After an initial statement, she thereafter adamantly refused to discuss the assassination. After that night, her career and health deteriorated in a downward spiral. She continued to tour for another eight years but never regained her popularity with audiences. She played to smaller and smaller houses and for one-week engagements rather than the two-week engagements she had previously enjoyed. Although she continued presenting *Our American Cousin,* she was aging and critics found that as an actress, her effectiveness was diminished. She contracted tuberculosis and died In Montclair, New Jersey on November 4, 1873 and is buried in Brooklyn, New York. She was forty-seven years old.

Harry Hawk remained loyal to Laura Keene and continued to tour with her as part of her company. He never achieved wide-spread fame as an actor but was a reliable journeyman ready to accept any role in any production. He successfully fought off alcoholism and spent almost fifty years touring in mostly forgettable dramas.

The highly respected John Dyott's career also slipped after the assassination as he found it difficult to adjust to changing public expectations. He ended his career by performing in outdated melodramas.

The building bought by John Ford was originally a church and he had it renovated into what became a thriving theater. Ford's Theater closed the night of the horrific crime and remained closed until 1968 when it was renovated and reopened as a theater. During the 2000's it was renovated again and reopened on February 12, 2009, in commemoration of Lincoln's 200th birthday. Today, the building houses a flourishing theater and a museum and together with the Peterson House, it is preserved as the Ford's Theater National Historic Site and is administered by the National Park Service.

THEODATE POPE

"I was born at midnight of February 2nd and 3rd – arriving before I was needed and greatly to my mother's resentment." My name is Theodate Pope. I was born into wealth and privilege in Salem, Ohio in 1867. Our home was located on Cleveland's "Millionaire's Row." In the two years following my birth, Mother deliberately brought on two miscarriages. As a very small child, one of my earliest memories is hearing her tell my father that she *"would not bear a child for him every year."* Needless to say, my mother's unorthodox, decidedly non-maternal declaration was indeed unusual for the time and was to have a profound effect on my view of the world. My parents were kind, intelligent, respected people who loved me but simply were disinterested in parenting.

"I have no memory at all of ever sitting in my mother's lap." My father was so occupied with business affairs that *"I was fifteen years old before he realized he was losing his child."* He was too busy building his career at the Cleveland Malleable Iron Co. to take much notice of me. The company was largely funded by the investments of Naugatuck, Connecticut philanthropist, John Howard Whittemore, Father became president of the company and an iron tycoon at age thirty-seven and our two families formed a close friendship that was to last the rest of our lives.

The search for a suitable, proper boarding school for me led my parents to enroll me at the prestigious Miss Porter's School for Young Ladies in Farmington, Connecticut, a school that had been established for educating the daughters of American aristocracy. I was very happy to be attending what to my mind was an aesthetically pleasing school. I also was very much taken with the architecture of the buildings that lined the main street of Farmington. Life for me at Miss Porter's School was both instructive and challenging. I was fortunate to be gifted with a clever mind and a talent for art and design. On the downside, I was encumbered with a strong, independent and rather opinionated nature. It was not at all unusual to find me questioning, arguing and debating my teachers over lessons and other instructional material. Ironically, at the same time I was disagreeing with my teachers, I desperately wanted their attention and approval in the hope that they would fill the void left by my disinterested parents. I was generally happy at Miss Porter's but was often troubled with the fatigue and depression which were to burden me my whole life.

One of my notable acts of establishing my independence had to do with my name. My parents named me Effie Brooks Pope. I found that sorry appellation to be totally unacceptable. At the age of nineteen, I declared that from that time forward, I would be addressed by the name of my grandmother, Theodate, a name which means "God's Gift." I thought the name Theodate to be a decidedly more dignified name than Effie. After all, my grandmother and I shared the same drive to *"see clearer into the invisible, spiritual part of life."* Further, Theodate could easily be mistaken for a male name which would be helpful if I ever decided to establish myself in a career. I steadfastly refused to answer to the name of Effie, and before long, I was addressed by everyone as Theodate.

After graduating from Miss Porter's School, as was *de rigueur* for children of the wealthy, I embarked on a two-year Grand Tour of Europe with my parents. We were accompanied by Howard Whittemore's son, Harris. I found myself entranced by the architectural styles I saw in England and could often be found with sketch book in hand drawing the likeness of a particularly lovely house or an interesting chimney. Harris was bent on wooing me into marriage but I wanted no part of it. *"The truth of the matter is the idea of marriage is totally repellent to me."* I liked Harris and thought him a fine young man but to me, marriage meant the end of my dreams. My mother's life as a socialite wife held no interest for me. I decidedly did not wish to follow in her footsteps as I loathed the luxurious and empty existence of the exceedingly rich. My wish was to build a farmhouse in the country where I could nurture young orphans in need of love. After much soul searching, I turned Harris down but placed great value on continuing our friendship. Depression, which had been a persistent battle during much of my early life, raised its ugly head again. It had been exacerbated by the stress caused by Harris' relentless pursuit of me.

Ironically, it was during this period of depression, that Father and I grew very close. We spent innumerable hours visiting Parisian salons and galleries searching for paintings and other *objets d'art.* We both became devotees of the impressionist painters, especially Monet, and Father's first purchase was Monet's *View of Cap d'Antibes.* There were many more purchases to follow and in addition to Monet, his acquisitions also included paintings by Degas, and the Americans James Whistler and Mary Cassatt. Father would eventually be among the first major American collectors of Impressionism.

Our excursions led me, more than ever, to be determined to design my own farmhouse. I was inspired by what I saw in the English countryside and diligently sketched out my ideas. *"Hope is very lovely in its place but if I do not act I shall wake some morning to find myself middle aged and sorrowing because I have not tried to make the world I touch a little better."* To my surprise, Father suggested I consider a career in architecture. I found this idea to be very appealing but was worried by the fact that the field of architecture was strictly for men. Women had begun making early forays into previously exclusive male occupations like medicine, but female architects were almost unheard of. I was troubled by the thought that if I were to pursue a career in architecture, I would be considered *"rather mannish and of all the unlovely things in the world an unwomanly woman is the worst."*

Upon my return to Farmington, and with my parents' financial backing and blessing, I bought a house just down the road from Miss Porter's School. The house was built in 1725 and badly in need of renovation. I planned and designed the update of the house and expanded the property by building a second house on the site for my parents and servants. It was not unusual for women to be involved in restoring old houses but what was unusual was that I directed and supervised every minute detail of the restoration, dealing with workmen and ordering them about to ensure the work was done to my specifications. My goal was to make the cottage appear as it might have a century earlier. I succeeded in doing just that and followed up this success by designing and building several more houses and schools.

A few years later, Father announced his retirement, and I convinced my parents that Farmington would be an ideal retirement location for them. I selected a lovely building site right behind my house. I drew up the plans and designs for the house and the blueprint for Hill-Stead House was born. My plan was to design a house that would be comfortable and yet be an architectural masterpiece. My parents by now had an extensive art collection that included Whistler, Monet, Degas, Manet and Cassatt. My design for the interior of the house would showcase that collection. I wanted wide halls and large rooms which opened into each other and followed the modern example of Frank Lloyd Wright. Like Wright, I felt it was important to connect the house to the landscape and to let nature and the texture of the materials themselves become the elements of design. The exterior would be of Colonial Revival style and would somewhat resemble Mount Vernon with two-story columns across an open portico. The southern charm of the house would be accented by a herd of Guernsey cows that would produce the highest quality milk and butterfat.

Female architects were still almost unheard of. There were no schools that accepted women architecture students so Father planned a course of study for me. He arranged for me to study art history privately at Princeton even though I actually was not enrolled as a student. When my education at Princeton was completed, he arranged for me to work with a respected architectural firm which would provide me with the necessary support to design and build Hill-Stead. My completed project was immensely successful, but like my earlier ventures, left me exhausted. *"For years I have been keen on architecture and felt that the ugliness of our buildings actually menaced my happiness and felt breathlessly that I must help in the cause of good architecture. But I have wrung my soul dry in that direction over Father's house."*

I eventually regained my strength and went on to many other projects one of which was Hop Brook School. My old beau, Harris Whittemore, a philanthropist like his father, commissioned the school for the children of foreign laborers. The school spoke to my desire to help the less fortunate and I created a warm and loving environment for the children to learn. Most public schools at the time were multi-storied square buildings with rows of windows and asphalt playgrounds. I designed Hop Brook to fit into its New England landscape with a spacious front lawn and arched doorways. I included a cozy fireplace in my design and created a separate entrance for the kindergartners with the letters ABC over the entrance.

Father died suddenly of a cerebral hemorrhage in 1913 and I took his death very hard. I resolved to build a preparatory school in his memory. His death also furthered my continuing interest in psychic phenomena. The general public also had high interest as the loss of life brought on by the Great War gave impetus to reach out to lost loved ones. Ouija boards and after-dinner séances were very popular and the beliefs in psychic phenomena and in an afterlife were widespread in America and Britain.

Theodate Pope

My unremitting interest in psychic phenomena led me to book passage on the *Lusitania* which was bound for the British Isles. I was accompanied by my maid, Emily Robinson, and a young colleague, Edwin Friend. Edwin and I were hoping to form a new psychical organization and were sailing to England with the expectation of gaining support for the project in Europe. The year was 1914 and the world was at war. Germany had warned that all ships, military and civilian alike, sailing near the British Isles would be considered targets. Most passengers on the *Lusitania* were apprehensive but not really afraid as it was widely believed that no country would have the audacity to actually torpedo civilian vessels. The idea of a torpedo attack on a civilian liner was simply incomprehensible. Furthermore, as we neared England, surely the British would send an escort for our protection. We were wrong! As the *Lusitania* sailed at a slow eighteen knots or about twenty-five miles per hour into the war zone near southern Ireland, the ship suffered a direct hit by a torpedo. That which had been the source of many nervous jokes and laughter throughout the entire crossing had become reality. The scene was one of chaos and death. Despite the pandemonium, Edwin helped Emily and me put on life jackets. He jumped overboard first. From the steeply listing deck I fearfully looked down at the churning ocean below. The angry, dark sea seemed to be so very far, far away. Desperately, I reached for Emily's hand and together we followed Edwin into the ice cold water. I would never see either one again. Something hit me hard in the head and I was knocked unconscious. I later learned that I was pulled from the sea by two sailors on the rescue ship, *Julia,* and so survived. My two traveling companions did not. One thousand, one hundred and ninety-eight passengers died that day. It took only eighteen minutes for the *Lusitania* to disappear beneath the sea.

Still reeling from my ordeal, I returned to Farmington and renewed my dream of building a school for boys that would be a memorial to my father. It had to be perfect in every way. Anything less was simply not acceptable. I envisioned a campus that would resemble a New England town. My creative process began with seeing in my mind's eye *"buildings completely surrounding the Village Green at Avon – none of which existed at the time. They began moving, coming forward and receding, shifting slightly until one of them backed off. I eventually omitted that building in my drawings."* I was also very involved and particular regarding every aspect of the curriculum. Some considered my ideas to be radical, but I was adamant that the curriculum foster in our students initiative, willpower and individual thinking. I felt it imperative that the students be required to spend a significant portion of their time in community service as this is a primary tool in building good character. Work on the school continued for the next ten years and on September 27, 1927, Avon Old Farms was ready to welcome its first students.

Over the years, I had acquired many close, noteworthy friends, among them William and Henry James, Mary Cassatt and Teddy Roosevelt's sister, Anna Roosevelt. Anna had long ago introduced me to John Wallace Riddle, but we were just friends. John and I stayed in touch over the years, and then to the surprise of everyone, at the age of forty-nine, I married him. John was a man of superior intelligence, and most importantly to me, was very supportive of my architectural career. He graduated from Harvard in 1886 and was a graduate of Columbia Law School. He was a diplomat who was fluent in six languages. We traveled to many countries as John's diplomatic posts took us to Turkey, Egypt, Romania, Russia, and Argentina. I affectionately called John "Totem Pole" in reference to his 6'2" height. In return, he referred to me as "Dearest of Geniuses."

Back in 1914, I had adopted a two-year old boy named Gordon Brockaway. At the time, it was unheard of for a single woman to adopt a child. John moved to Hill-Stead to live with me and Gordon, and along with my mother and servants, we were a happy household. Heartbreakingly, just a short two years later, Gordon contracted polio and died. We were all devastated by the tragedy. In 1917 and again in 1918, John and I took in two more orphan boys whom we raised as foster children. Between our overseas posts, I continued with my architectural career. Tragically, on December 7, 1941, the same day that President Roosevelt declared war on Japan, my John collapsed at Hill-Stead and died.

Once again, the world was embroiled in a world war and in 1944 I turned Avon Old Farms School over to the army and the buildings were converted into The Old Farms Convalescent Hospital for blind veterans. I was very pleased to have my beautiful buildings used for such a worthy cause.

EPILOGUE

In August 1946, Theodate Pope died after a long battle with cystitis and finally, kidney failure. She left a legacy of helping to further the cause of women's rights. In 1916 she was licensed as an architect in New York and in 1918 was accepted into the American Institute of Architects, only the fifth woman in the entire country to do so. The Old Farms Convalescent Hospital gained national prominence due in large part to its magnificent architecture. In 1948, the campus was returned to its original intention and the school reopened. Today, Old Farms School houses four hundred boys in grades 9 through 12. Its buildings are considered to be among the most beautiful and innovative in the country. Some of Theodate Pope's other projects include the building and restoration of several houses including Theodore Roosevelt's birthplace in New York City, the Hop Brook School in Naugatuck, Connecticut, Westover School in Middlebury, Connecticut, and even a golf course.

Her most lasting contribution is Hill-Stead House which has been designated a National Historic Site. It is toured by thirty thousand visitors annually. In addition to designing Hill-Stead, she also built three houses on the property for Hill-Stead workers. Her will stipulates that Hill-Stead House become a museum and memorial to her parents "for the benefit and enjoyment of the public." The will further stipulates that the house and contents remain intact and not be moved, lent or sold. Today, the collection at the thirty thousand square foot Hill-Stead Museum stands unique as its collection of paintings, drawings, photographs, furnishings, sculptures, decorative arts, rugs and textiles remain intact in its original domestic setting. All of the buildings on the property but one are still standing today as enduring testimony to this preeminent pioneer of women architects.

WARTIME

SYBIL LUDINGTON

We live in very trying, dangerous times. The war has been going on for almost two years and it is very difficult for all of us. Father is away much of the time serving with the Continental Army under General George Washington. Tending the farm and the gristmill is left to mother, me and those of my younger brothers and sisters who are old enough to help care for the animals and collect the chickens' eggs. I try to help mother as much as I can sewing, cooking, knitting, spinning, weaving and helping take care of the little ones. My name is Sybil Ludington. I am sixteen years old and live with my father, Colonel Henry Ludington, my mother Abigail, and my ten younger brothers and sisters in Kent County, New York. Our farm is quite prosperous and Father is very well respected in the community. Two years ago we were friends with all our neighbors, but nowadays we cannot be certain as to which of our neighbors are in favor of the rebellion and are ready to fight for freedom and independence and which neighbors remain loyal to the King. The atmosphere is heavy with tension, unease and mistrust.

Father's military career began when he was just seventeen. In 1756 he enlisted in the 2nd Regiment of Connecticut troops in service of the King. He fought in the French and Indian War and Royal Governor of New York, William Tyron, appointed him Captain of the Fredericksburgh

Regiment of Militia in Duchess County. However, in the ensuing years, Father's loyalty to the King slowly eroded and after much soul-searching, in 1773 he resigned his commission in favor of the Revolutionary cause.

In 1776, he was appointed to the Patriot's Duchess County militia with the rank of Colonel. His regiment was assigned to cover the most direct and likely British route from the coast on Long Island Sound to the upper New York-Connecticut border. This area was coveted by the British as it was of prime strategic importance. The four hundred soldiers of the regiment led by Father were involved in many skirmishes. The territory was crowded with Tory supporters and subjected to guerrilla tactics by the always dangerous mercenary 'cowboys and skinners.' The 'cowboys' favored the Tories and the 'skinners' favored the Patriots, but both groups were unscrupulous and stole from, tortured and murdered the local farmers no matter where their loyalties fell. Father and his soldiers were so successful in protecting the region and preventing the British from obtaining supplies, that British General William Howe put a price on Father's head of three hundred English guineas if he were to be captured dead or alive.

On April 25, 1777, British General William Tyron and his force of two thousand men sailed up Long Island Sound to Fairfield, Connecticut. They arrived with twenty transports and six warships. The next day they marched on to their objective, Danbury, Connecticut, the site where the Continental Army stored their supplies. As the British moved through the town, they marked the doors of the Loyalists with chalk marks. They then set out to destroy the unmarked homes by setting them afire. By four o'clock that afternoon, several of the Army storehouses and three private dwellings had been destroyed. The loss of the storehouses was devastating to the Patriot's cause as they contained "foodstuffs such as flour, beef, pork, sugar, molasses, coffee, rice, wheat, corn, wine and rum. Hospital cots and tents were also stored there, along with clothing, shoes and cooking utensils." The loss of the storehouses was disastrous. As they plundered Danbury, the British soldiers were careful to not get rid of the rum but rather to help themselves to it freely, and the drunken men lit many more fires until most of the town was ablaze.

Meanwhile, after months of fighting, and unaware of the brewing disaster in Danbury, Father and his men had been given permission to return to their farms. The men were needed at home as it was time for the spring crops to be planted. I remember so clearly the night of April 26, 1777. It was raining very hard, but we were all snug and warm as the family gathered around the hearth and I helped Mother clear our supper dishes. Father was telling us about the supplies and medicines he and his men had secured when we heard the sound of rapidly approaching hoof beats and then insistent pounding on our door. Who could it be at this late hour? The clock on the mantle indicated it was nine o'clock. On our doorstep, we found a drenched, exhausted, muddied young messenger sent from Danbury to notify Father that it was imperative he quickly assemble his men and come to the aid of the beleaguered town. The militia would muster immediately upon being apprised of the situation but they were scattered throughout the region at home on their farms. How could they be warned of the crisis? The messenger was exhausted and unfamiliar with the area. He could become lost, captured or worse. On the other hand, my horse Star, (aptly named because of the white patch on his nose), and I were thoroughly familiar with the territory's woods and trails and had ridden over them many times.

Taking a deep breath, I volunteered to ride to the farms and alert the militia volunteers about the imminent danger to Danbury and to inform them that they were to muster at Col. Ludington's immediately. At first, Father and Mother insisted that I would do no such thing. I was just sixteen years old, a mere girl and it was much too dangerous. They pointed out that it was a very dark moonless night, a blinding rain was falling and besides possible Redcoats, the woods were full of the always dangerous 'cowboys and skinners.' I protested that there simply was no one else. The messenger could ride no further, and Father needed to remain at home to mobilize the men when they arrived. And so with many misgivings on the part of my parents, (and secretly on my part as well) it was decided. I would be the one to sound the alarm.

I quickly got myself ready for what I knew would be an arduous, perilous ride. I dressed myself warmly in my wool cloak and hat, tucked my breeches into my boots and ran to the barn to saddle up Star. And we were off. I was filled with dread and apprehension, but I knew I had to do this. The night was inky black and the torrential rain quickly made me feel like a drowned rat. Although I was exceedingly familiar with the woods and fields, everything looked very different to me at night. I grabbed a stout tree limb thinking I could use it as protection if I ran into any marauders or British spies. I could also use it to bang on the front doors of the militiamen so they would hear my shouts above the noise of the rain and thunder.

Muddied and soaked to the skin, the rain streaming down my cheeks and off my nose, I at last reached the home of the first militiaman on my route. With thick bough in hand, I furiously banged on the farmhouse door and shouted the warning that the British were burning Danbury and to meet at Colonel Ludington's right away. I then rode off to the second farmhouse, and the third and so on throughout the night. In this way, I traveled south to Mahopac and north to Stormville, before at last, near dawn the next day, I finally returned home. Altogether, Star and I traveled about forty miles round trip. By the time we finally arrived home, I was chilled to the bone, drenched and miserable, my fingers and toes aching with the cold. And I was tired. So tired. The sight of four hundred militiamen assembled in our yard ready to march to battle and rescue Danbury revived my energy and cheered me considerably.

I later learned from Father that the Ludington troops marched on to Danbury where they joined the forces commanded by Generals Benedict Arnold and David Wooster. Unfortunately, they ultimately arrived too late to save the town but the out-numbered militia did manage to surprise the British. During the ensuing Battle of Ridgefield, they forced General Tyron and his men to retreat all the way back to Long Island Sound to the waiting ships that had brought them.

Shortly afterwards, I was the recipient of a singular honor. General George Washington himself, came to our farm to thank me personally for my contribution to the War for Independence. Imagine me, a sixteen-year-old girl being so honored by that great man. I will never forget that day.

EPILOGUE

After her historic ride, Sybil led a quiet, unremarkable life. In 1784, at age twenty-three, she married farmer and innkeeper Edmond Ogden and they had one son. Edmond Ogden's revolutionary service included membership in the Connecticut Continentals and naval duty under John Paul Jones aboard the *Bonhomme Richard.* The family lived quietly in Unadilla, New York and after Edmond's death Sybil continued on as innkeeper. She died in 1839 at the age of seventy-seven.

Historians have credited Sybil's ride as being equal in importance to the outcome of the war as the famous ride of Paul Revere. There were however, three significant differences. Longfellow's wonderful poem describing the ride of Paul Revere insured the silversmith's fame and lasting legacy. Although several poems celebrating Sybil's important contribution to the war effort were written, none received the large audience that Longfellow's beautiful poem enjoyed. Secondly, Paul Revere rode his horse twenty miles to warn the colonists that "The British are coming! The British are coming!" Sybil's ride encompassed forty miles, twice as far as the ride of Paul Revere. Lastly, unlike Paul Revere, Sybil Ludington was not caught.

Today, historical markers tracing Sybil's route posted by the New York State Education Department can be seen throughout eastern Putnam County, New York. As part of the Bicentennial, the National Women's Party adopted Sybil Ludington as a symbol in the campaign for the Equal Rights Amendment. There have been several children's books written about her exploits as well as an opera which was performed in Manhattan in 1993. In 1975, she was honored on an eight-cent postage stamp in the "Contributions to the Cause" United States Bicentennial Series. She was one of only thirty-five women to be so honored up to that time.

Most interesting and unusual is the story of the larger-than-life statue of Sybil Ludington sculptured by Anna Hart Huntington and erected near Carmel, New York. The statue depicts a defiant Sybil riding side-saddle on her horse, rein in one hand and a twig held as a whip in the other hand. The statue is of a rebellious, courageous girl who is quite literally foaming at the mouth. It seems that foundry workers accidently left part of the plaster mold inside Sybil's head when the bronze was cast and over time the plaster leaked through the metal giving her the appearance of foaming at the mouth. The statue has been cleaned many times but the "foam" eventually always reappears. Smaller versions of the statue can be seen on the grounds of the Daughters of the American Revolution building in Washington, D.C. and on the grounds of the public library in Danbury, Connecticut.

The Sybil Ludington 50-kilometer foot race has been held every April since 1979. The hilly ultramarathon race approximates Sybil's historic route and finishes near her statue in Carmel.

It should also be noted that there is something of a mystery surrounding the correct spelling of Sybil's name. Although it is customary for historians and biographers to spell her name "Sybil," the name on her tombstone in Patterson, New York is spelled "Sybbell." To add to the puzzlement, on her application for a Revolutionary War pension, she signed her name “Sebal,” yet her sister Mary spelled it “Sebil.” Adding to the riddle, the 1880 census lists her as “Sibel,” while other documents record her as “Cybil.” Confusion reigns.

MARY KATHERINE GODDARD

From the long perspective of my seventy-eight years, I reflect on my life with a gallimaufry of emotions. Do I still feel angry? Somewhat. Bitter? Perhaps, a little. Disappointed? Certainly. Proud of my accomplishments? Most assuredly. My name is Mary Katherine Goddard. I was born in 1738 to Dr. Giles and Sarah Goddard. Father was a physician and also the postmaster in Groton and New London, Connecticut. Mother was an unusually learned and erudite woman, well-educated in both Latin and French. She saw to it that I and my brother William, two years my junior, received classical educations. It was under her tutelage that we learned to read and appreciate Shakespeare, Pope and Swift. Due to his gender, William's schooling was assured, but my parents saw to it that I attended the New London Public School as well, where girls could study Latin, French and simple mathematics when the facilities were not needed for the boys.

When Father became incapacitated with gout, Mother assumed his postmaster duties and made arrangements for William to be apprenticed to New Haven printer, James Parker. Father's demise in 1757 left us heartbroken but financially secure. The three of us moved to Providence, Rhode Island in 1762, and Mother gave my twenty-two year old brother, William, three hundred pounds from Father's estate to purchase a printing press and finance the publishing of a newspaper, the *Providence Gazette and Country Journal*. The customary domestic pursuits of young ladies did not hold much interest for me and so I happily worked in the shop as a volunteer typesetter, printer and journalist. I worked diligently "*more from sheer exuberance and pleasure than from necessity*" meanwhile observing Mother's superb managerial skills. The *Gazette* was the first newspaper in the colony and exerted much influence on our readers.

William, Mother and I worked long hours, but despite our best efforts, we were faced with lagging circulation problems and in 1765 were forced to temporarily close down the newspaper. William chose this inopportune time to try to advance his flagging career by moving to Philadelphia. Again, with Mother's financial help, he joined with others and opened another print shop and started a new newspaper, the *Pennsylvania Chronicle and Universal Advertiser*. One of the paper's investors was Benjamin Franklin.

In the meantime, back in Rhode Island, although it was no longer economically feasible to print a newspaper, it was left to Mother and me to keep the Providence printing business going, and that we did. We printed broadsides, pamphlets, and stationery. We also printed legal blanks and forms for businesses which eliminated the time-consuming process of hand-copying. The Sarah Goddard and Company shop also printed an almanac which provided farmers and housewives with information about times of sunrises and sunsets, phases of the moon and tide schedules as well as blank pages for journal keeping. In addition to her printing duties, my clever and industrious mother also ran the Providence post office.

With little consideration of our needs and desires, William summoned Mother and me to Philadelphia to help him manage and operate his newest newspaper enterprise. Although William was the youngest member of our family, he was the "man of the house" and mother and I reluctantly acceded to his demands. In 1768, Mother sold our Providence business and we followed William to Philadelphia.

William was passionate and vocal about his dislike of England's iron rule of the colonies. However, his unruly behavior and volatile short temper continually kept him at odds with the other patriot activists. He was jailed frequently for his public outbursts and for his rabble-rousing articles in the *Chronicle* against the British. He spent much of his time frequently traveling from Georgia to Massachusetts espousing his radical ideas leaving the publishing of the paper to Mother and me. It wasn't long before my reputation as a steady, responsible and meticulous printer and fair-minded editor began to grow and the reputation of the *Chronicle* grew with it. After Mother's death in 1770, it was often left to me to run the shop alone under William's name. My brother was either traveling or too involved with politics to concern himself with the everyday business of running the *Chronicle.* I can say with pride, that I followed the excellent business practices I had learned from Mother and our "shop became one of the largest in the colonies." It was later said that the *Chronicle* was the best edited pre-Revolutionary newspaper in Philadelphia.

To the displeasure of the British, the patriots' cause was heavily favored by the *Chronicle.* The British retaliated by instituting a burdensome tax on the delivery of the paper by the Crown Post. The Crown's postmaster also effectively disrupted communication between the colonies by destroying out-of-town newspapers and blocking mail delivery, thereby depriving us of critical news and information. Private letters were opened, read and censored. This disruption in the lines of communication finally resulted in, and was the direct cause of, the failure of the *Chronicle.* William was to later exact his revenge on the British postal system.

Unfortunately, William's irascible, short-tempered personality and frequent run-ins with patriot leadership made impossible any feasible friendship with the brilliant Benjamin Franklin. Friendship with any of the other leaders of the burgeoning patriot movement was likewise deemed hopeless. And so in 1772, William was on the move again. He had few friends and was besieged by creditors. Leaving me in charge of the business, he relocated to Baltimore where he hoped to start a third newspaper. *The Maryland Journal and Baltimore Advertiser* appeared for the first time on August 20, 1773.

Again I was summoned, this time to Baltimore, to assist William in the print shop and with the publishing of the *Journal.* As I was just a woman alone and subject to the "protection" of my brother, I had no choice but to reluctantly sell the Philadelphia print shop the following year and follow William to Baltimore. The *Journal* was Baltimore's first local newspaper and I worked diligently to make it a success. To my mind, it was imperative that the newspaper publish the truth and do it in a way that informed and educated its readers. Under my watchful eye, the *Journal* became one of the best newspapers in the colonies. Our motto was adopted from a Latin couplet by Horace which when translated read: "He carries every point who blends the useful with the agreeable, amusing the reader while he instructs him."

During this period, William was very busy with his political activities. The colonies were in desperate need of a postal system and the Committee of Correspondence meeting in Boston urged that an independent national postal system be created. William was asked to help in its planning and design. The new intercolonial postal system was to be in direct opposition to the postal system run by the British. William felt very strongly that the new "Constitutional Post" be free of the Crown restraints that had resulted in the failure of the *Chronicle.* He brilliantly designed a new postal system founded on the principles of open communication without governmental interference and which fostered a free exchange of ideas. By the time the Continental Congress met in Philadelphia, William's postal system had already proven a great success. Thirty post offices were operating between Portsmouth, New Hampshire and Williamsburg, Pennsylvania. The formation of the new mail system was critical as it served as the main conduit for disseminating information throughout the colonies. The mail system also spread and increased the circulation of newspapers which, in turn, was instrumental in raising the reputation of the *Journal* with its readers throughout the colonies. William hoped to be appointed Postmaster General when the government of the new United States was formed.

Due to my brother's long absences, I was finally able to establish myself as the publisher of the *Journal.* On May 10, 1775, "Baltimore: Published by M.K. Goddard, at the Printing Office in Market-Street, next Door above Dr. John Stevenson's" appeared on the paper's masthead. The *Journal* was the only newspaper published in Baltimore during the Revolution and it was known as a valuable source of news.

I felt rather conflicted about William. I was proud of his passionate desire for freedom from England. At the same time, I was appalled by his obnoxious behavior and violent quarrels with other patriot leaders. But mostly, I was secretly pleased that his frequent travels for the patriots' cause, left me alone to run the *Journal* as I saw fit. Under my editorship, the *Journal* expressed the colonists' desire for freedom. The War for Independence was being set in motion. I am proud that the *Journal* was the first newspaper to report on the momentous events in Lexington and Concord, Massachusetts. The editorial of June 14, 1775 proclaimed, "The ever memorable 19th of April gave a conclusive answer to the questions of American freedom. What think ye of Congress now? That day … evidenced that Americans would rather die than live as slaves!"

1775 was a landmark year for the colonies and for me personally as well. The fight for independence had begun. It was also during this year that I was appointed the first postmistress in Colonial America under the leadership of Postmaster General Benjamin Franklin. The dual position of postmistress and publisher put me in the enviable position of being at the very center of information, a position I relished. I had the advantage of being able to publish news more quickly than my competitors. These were very newsworthy but discordant, dangerous times and I fearlessly and accurately published news of the events as they unfolded.

I disagreed with my brother about the function of a newspaper. He used the paper as an outlet for rabble-rousing articles that voiced his own views. I thought that newspapers should report the news fairly in a manner that informed and educated its readers. I reported and commented on the British reaction to American protests and on the blockade of Boston Harbor and matter-of-factly described the cruelty of British soldiers. I did my best to bolster the courage of the patriots. I appealed to women that they had a role to play as well. In an essay I wrote in 1775 titled, "A Friend to Liberty and the Fair," I urged women to practice frugality and to raise flax and wool which would lead to greater independence from the Crown.

Newspapers were becoming essential for communication and circulation quickly doubled as colonists were hungry for news of the expanding conflict. I tried my best to keep an objective and professional voice in reporting events. Unlike my brother, I did not want the *Journal* to be a reflection of my own opinions. I consistently insisted that our readers be informed of the latest war news with facts, not rumors.

The war was causing considerable hardship throughout the colonies. Inflation was a big problem and was hitting the pocketbooks of my subscribers. I allowed them to pay for their subscriptions by either cash or goods including "Beef, Pork, or any kind of Animal Food, Butter, Hog's Lard, Tallow, Bees-Wax, Flour, Wheat, Rye, Indian Corn… tann'd Sheepskins, brown Linen… and Cotton Rags." Due to the new postal system, newspapers were no longer subject to censorship.

However, wartime shortages of paper sometimes resulted in my having to print the Journal on small sheets of paper instead of the standard ten-by-fifteen size paper, but publish I did. I also allowed patriot propagandists to submit essays. Thomas Paine's "Common Sense" appeared in two installments.

It was difficult to keep the paper operating during these times of turmoil and many other newspapers folded. There was much confusion over whether the British or Colonial government was in control of Baltimore. Keeping the mail running was imperative and was also a huge problem. The colonial government had very little money and I often paid the post riders out of my own personal funds.

On July 4, 1776, events came to a head. Independence from Great Britain was proclaimed in Philadelphia when the Declaration of Independence was adopted by the Continental Congress. John Hancock, President of the Congress and Charles Thomson, Secretary, courageously signed the handwritten parchment document. Treason! Imprisonment! Hanging! All possible outcomes for the signers of the seditious document. It took six months before all the potential signatories mustered up their courage to reveal their identities by signing. For those six months, copies of the Declaration of Independence were circulated among the colonies with only the Hancock and Thomson signatures.

On January 18, 1777, the Continental Congress required that "an authentic copy of the Declaration of Independence, with the names of the members of Congress subscribing to the same be sent to each of the United States." Summoning their courage, each delegate, at last, signed the instrument. Now, with all fifty-six signatures affixed to the document, I was honored to be chosen by the Continental Congress to be the first to print the Declaration of Independence with the names of all the document's signers.

For me, it was prodigiously gratifying to have my efforts of fairmindedness and integrity recognized and appreciated by our Founding Fathers in this way. I understood very well the importance of this event as well as the risks I would be taking in printing the document. England considered the Declaration a treasonous crime punishable by hanging for both its signers and printers. I proudly and fearlessly typeset and printed the historic one thousand three hundred and thirty-seven word document. With a defiant flourish, I signed the piece with my full name instead of just my initials as I customarily did. With the identities of all the signers now revealed, our new country had fully declared itself; there was no turning back.

Perhaps it was due to jealousy of my success or possibly he simply was trying to evade his creditors, but William returned to Baltimore ostensibly to assist with the newspaper. Although I was pleased to see my brother, I was not happy with his involvement with the *Journal.* The paper was vital and well-respected and William's interference led to frequent disagreements between us. As time went on we became embroiled in ferocious recurrent arguments. The quarrels were so bitter and acrimonious, we eventually became completely alienated from each other.

Things would not turn in my favor. William's name was added to the colophon and my name was dropped. By late 1784, our venomous arguments had caused the deterioration of our relationship to such a point that we each published rival almanacs for the year 1785. In his habitual bombastic style, William attacked both my almanac and my character. Finally, in 1785, after forcing me to accept a pitiful sum for the *Journal,* my ties to the newspaper I had helped found were forever severed. My career as a printer and publisher abruptly came to a close. I was furious with William and determined to have nothing more to do with him. I even refused to attend his wedding. I filed five lawsuits against him, but it all came to naught.

Unfortunately, things were to get even worse for me. As the first woman ever appointed to a Federal office, I had used the *Journal* to notify readers of changes in daily and weekly post schedules, list unclaimed letters and promulgate Baltimore Post Office regulations. Back In 1774, I had established a postal delivery service and ran an advertisement for a mailman in the *Journal*. Nevertheless, when Mr. Washington's government came into power, to William's great disappointment, he was passed over and Samuel Osgood was appointed the new Postmaster General.

Unfortunately, Mr. Osgood preferred one of his supporters, rather than me, to serve as Baltimore's postmaster. He erroneously claimed that the newly expanded position now required a great deal of travel, more "than a woman could undertake." Despite the fact that I had held the position for fourteen years, had handled the presses, loaded books and boxes, paid for the post riders out of my own pocket during the years of wartime hardships, and supervised the early operation of the postal delivery system, I was now deemed inadequate for the job. It was gratifying that two hundred and thirty Baltimore citizens demanded my reinstatement, but it did no good. I wrote President Washington reminding him of my loyal service and claiming that "my post office remained the most punctual and regular of any upon the Continent." Unfortunately, the President was not sympathetic to my cause replying that prudence dictated that he follow the advice of his Postmaster General.

I was never paid for my years of service during the war when there was little money in the Continental treasury. I was never reimbursed for the advances I made to the post riders out of my own pocket. Although my conduct as postmistress had always been exemplary, I was now a woman on her own after being unjustly forced out of two jobs that I had performed admirably. So, yes, I am disappointed and distressed about the unjust way things turned out for me. On the other hand, I am fully aware of my important and valuable contributions to the cause of freedom and walk with my head held high with dignity and self-respect.

EPILOGUE

After the loss of her dual occupations, Mary Katherine Goddard continued to live in Baltimore where she was the proprietor of a bookstore from 1784 until she retired in 1810. She never married and died in 1816 at the age of seventy-eight and is buried in Baltimore. In her will, she freed her slave, Belinda Starling, who was her personal assistant during her later years. Miss Starling was also the beneficiary of Goddard's meager estate.

Most historians have credited this unsung and forgotten hero of the American Revolution as being instrumental to its ultimate success. During the tumultuous years between 1775 and 1784, she never missed printing an edition of the *Journal.* Her diligence and courage set a standard for the importance of freedom of speech. Due to her fearless printing of one of America's most revered signed documents, these singular signers are today still rightfully honored for their bravery. It is ironic, that as the fame of these courageous men rose, Mary Katherine Goddard's name sank into obscurity.

Although she consistently lost her battles with her brother and the government for the right of women to pursue a career, she was and should be remembered as a pioneer and trailblazer in the fight for women's rights.

Her petition to Postmaster General Samuel Osgood can be seen in the National Archives Building in Washington, D.C. A copy of the Declaration of Independence printed by Mary Katherine Goddard is located in the Maryland Hall of Records. The Omaha chapter of the Daughters of the American Revolution have named their chapter in her honor.

The postal system designed and implemented by the erratic William Goddard ultimately became the postal system still in use today. In 1792, William relinquished the editorship of the *Journal* and returned to Rhode Island where he entered politics.

BELLE BOYD

Hello boys. My, but don't y'all look handsome in your army uniforms. Gray is such a manly color. Now, now, don't look away. I saw you take those furtive glances in my direction. I'm not embarrassed by them; in fact, I welcome them. I am well aware that my face is comely and my form pleasing and am mindful that I am regularly noticed by men and envied by women. Throughout the countryside, I am considered as fine a horsewoman as can be found anywhere. My name is Belle Boyd and I am seventeen years old.

My childhood in Martinsburg, Virginia (now West Virginia) was pleasant but unremarkable. My family did not possess great wealth but we were very comfortable and my parents saw to it that I, and my brothers and sisters, were provided with good educations. However, my family's circumstances were dramatically altered with the onset of the war. The men in my family, uncles, cousins and even my forty-five-year-old father all enlisted in the Confederate Army. Father served in that section of the army known as the Stonewall Brigade.

For me, the difficulties became readily evident the day a band of no-good Yankee soldiers ransacked my family home. You see, my room was decorated with Confederate flags and everyone in town knew it. The Union soldiers heard about my patriotic decor and came to investigate.

Mother and I stood by, silently fuming, as drunken "bluecoats" smashed windows, tore down pictures and searched our house looking for southern souvenirs. Then they took it a step too far. The soldiers pulled out a big Union flag and began climbing a ladder that led to our roof with the intention of flying their odious banner from there. Mother was furious. She angrily called out, *"Men, every member of this household will die before that flag is raised over us."* The soldiers responded by flinging curses at Mother and one soldier actually had the temerity to push her aside. Incensed by the sheer effrontery of this action, *"I could stand it no longer; my indignation was aroused beyond control.... I drew out my Colt 1849 pocket pistol and shot him."* Well, wouldn't you have done the same? *"He was carried away mortally wounded and soon after expired."*

In the aftermath, a hearing was held and I was exonerated, but after that, sentries were posted outside our house and were instructed to keep close tabs on me. I had no objection to the close supervision of the sentries. It wasn't long before I had become very well acquainted with many of these soldiers. As I pointed out, I am quite decorative, extremely feminine, and with just minimum effort on my part, attract the attentions of men. One of my many rivals described me as *"the fastest girl in Virginia or anywhere else for that matter."* I also happen to have legs that other women may only dream about. Can I help it if my fine turn of ankle appears from under my petticoats when mounting my horse or dismounting from a carriage? I like to be noticed and customarily wear rich greens and reds and favor feathers in my hats. Needless to say, among my many admirers, were a number of Yankee soldiers and it wasn't long before they began letting slip little snippets of information.

And so began my career in espionage. I carefully wrote down every tidbit of intelligence I learned from the soldiers to pass on to my hero, Stonewall Jackson or to "Jeb" Stuart. I was pretty ignorant of the precautions that should be taken with messages and didn't realize I should use a cypher or at least try to disguise my handwriting. Of course, the inevitable happened and one of my notes reached the Union camp. The Colonel in command summoned me to Union headquarters. He read to me the 50th and 57th Articles of War which dealt with espionage and treason. He asked if I knew I could be sentenced to death. I resolutely refused to be frightened. After giving me a warning, he let me go. I made a full curtsy, turned to the other officers in the room and with dripping sarcasm said, *"Thank you gentlemen of the jury."* I gathered up my skirts and defiantly pirouetted out of the room. However, I did learn my lesson. I would have to be more careful in the future. I started using an old Negro named Sophie to help me get information to General Jackson. I hid my messages in a large, hollowed-out watch and in this way Sophie conveyed my notes to the General. I was thrilled by my adventures into spydom and was fired-up to do more.

I sought out Colonel Turner Ashby, head of military scouts in the Shenandoah Valley. He gave me many courier assignments and I put my considerable equestrian skills to work as I galloped through the back country carrying valuable military information. It was very exciting and I was happy to be of use to my beloved South. In late March, 1862, the fighting returned to Martinsburg and I left the Valley to see how I could help in my hometown. My route took me through the town of Winchester. As I rode past the railroad station, I was suddenly surrounded by a group of Union soldiers. Very politely, they begged my pardon and then summarily arrested me. They said I would need to accompany them to Baltimore. I maintained a serene demeanor, adjusted my lovely hat and assured the soldiers that nothing was going to happen to me in Baltimore. They took me to Eutaw House, one of the largest and best hotels in Baltimore which was to serve as my prison. I passed an agreeable week at the hotel charming my captors as officials puzzled over what to do with me. General Dix, the presiding officer, ruled that there was no specific evidence against me and said I could go. I made a deep curtsy, and with a nod, a sardonic smile and a swish of my petticoats, haughtily stalked away.

I planned to rejoin my family whom I thought to be living at the Fishback Hotel in Front Royal which was owned by my aunt and uncle. To my dismay, the hotel had been taken over by Union soldiers and my family had been moved to a small cottage. This was not what I wanted at all. I wanted to be where the action was, either at the hotel or in Richmond. I knew full well that in order to get what I wanted, I needed to find a man with the authority to grant my wishes. Straightaway, I went to the Union commander, General James Shields and asked for a pass to Richmond. He explained that if he gave me the pass I would need to go through General Jackson's lines and that he would not permit. With a twinkle in his eye, he told me that Jackson's army would be wiped out in a few days and I would then be able to get through to Richmond. I realized I had just been told valuable information. I quickly changed my mind about going to Richmond. Instead, using my feminine wiles, I set out to thoroughly enchant the General and his staff.

And so I met Captain Keily who was quickly and easily captivated by my "Je ne sais quoi." It turns out that Captain Keily was quite talkative. I am indebted to him for his *"remarkable effusions, some withered flowers, and last, not least, for a great deal of very important information."* From him I learned that a major Federal drive was imminent and that a war council was to be held in the parlor of my Aunt's hotel. It so happens, that directly over the parlor is a bedroom that has a closet with a knothole in the floor. I realized that if I lay down on the floor of the closet and put my ear next to the knothole, (I may have enlarged it a bit) I would be able to hear everything that was said in the room below. The Union officers gathered in the room, and over cigars and maps they plotted their strategies. I heard every word. I learned about placement of troops, tactics, names of officers, etc. I lay on the floor of that cramped space for hours devouring every nugget of information. The meeting lasted until one o'clock in the morning. After they left, I hurried back to the cottage where I quickly wrote down everything I remembered. I had learned my lesson and this time used a cypher to obfuscate my message.

It was imperative that this new information be delivered at once. Despite the early morning hour, I quietly saddled my horse Fleeter, and was soon galloping off towards the mountains where Colonel Ashby, Jackson's head spy, was camped. I rode alone across the moonlit fields, through country infested with Yankee scouts and guerillas. After riding hard for fifteen miles, I at last reached a house from which I had been told I could send an emergency message. I quickly dismounted and banged on the door demanding the sentry tell me where Ashby was encamped. An interior door opened and there stood Ashby himself. *"Good God! Miss Belle, is that you? Where did you come from? Have you dropped from the clouds or am I dreaming?"* Breathlessly, I told him all that I had learned and then quickly left to return to Front Royal before dawn broke and the bulk of the Union troops arrived. Now, that's what I call a good adventure.

A short time later, my cousin Alice and I, accompanied by my maid Eliza, set off for Winchester escorted by a besotted young Union lieutenant. While attending a party in Winchester, I was approached by a *"gentleman of high social standing."* He shoved several important papers into my hands saying that they must be delivered to General Jackson. The papers dealt with an impending clash between Northern and Southern forces. I gave some of the vital papers to my maid thinking that the Federals would not search a Negro. I placed the papers of lesser importance in a basket which I casually gave the infatuated lieutenant to carry for me. The final document, which was of critical importance, I carried myself.

Our small party got as far as the outskirts of Winchester when we were flagged down by a pair of detectives. We were arrested and taken to Union headquarters. I was getting rather experienced at this scenario and kept a steady head. I can't say the same for the Lieutenant who was completely flustered. Pretending reluctance. I reached into the basket still carried by the Lieutenant and solemnly gave the commanding Colonel the relatively unimportant message. The Colonel was furious with the disloyal actions of the Lieutenant with the result that the unlucky soldier remained under arrest while we girls were cleared of any charges of treachery. Of course, I still had the vital information in my possession.

In May of 1862, Jackson launched the critical campaign of the Shenandoah Valley. Although the Confederates had fewer than twenty thousand men while the Union army had several times that number, Jackson's plan was to upset the Union scheme to take Richmond. I sat in my parlor and thought about how I could be of assistance to the General. I was in possession of considerable information; the messages handed to me in Winchester, the military conference I had overheard in the hotel and the data I had gathered while at the various camps. I knew that General White was at Harpers Ferry, Generals Shields and Geary were near Front Royal and General Fremont was in the Valley. The plan was for the three divisions to unite. General Jackson had to be warned. I determined that I was the one to do so. Snatching my sunbonnet, off I went. *"I had on a dark-blue dress with a little fancy apron over it; and this contrast of colors, being visible at a great distance, made me far more conspicuous than was just then agreeable."* I made my way around the edges of the Union lines and past heavy guns and equipment. When I reached the open fields, the Union soldiers fired on me. Terrified, I threw myself off my horse onto the ground. I could feel the rifle balls *"flying thick and fast as I was caught in the cross fire of both Northern and Southern pickets. I shall never run again as I ran...on that day."* I scrambled over fences and crawled along the edges of hills and fields. Never have I felt such terror, yet I was determined to deliver my information.

At last, I approached the oncoming Southern line. I removed my white bonnet and joyfully waved it as a sign of encouragement. The soldiers shocked at the sight of a woman in such an exposed and dangerous spot, responded by returning my cheers. Exhausted, I fell to my knees. A soldier who turned out to be an old friend, Major Harry Douglas, came riding up; *"Great God, Belle, why are you here?"* Gasping for breath, I told him to go back quickly and tell General Jackson that the "*Yankee force is very small – one regiment of Maryland infantry, several pieces of artillery and several companies of cavalry. Tell him to charge right down and he will catch them all. I must hurry back. Goodbye. My love to all the dear boys – and remember, if you meet me in town you haven't seen me today."*

Spurred on by my information, Jackson and his men pushed through the town. According to the plan, the Union troops set fire to the bridge. The brave Confederate troops, defying the smoke and flames, pulled and kicked at the scorching timbers and tossed them into the water. Thanks to my timely information, the bridge was saved.

A week later, the southern forces abandoned Front Royal. I was denounced by a woman Union sympathizer as a dangerous enemy. I was arrested and my house was surrounded by sentries. Here, we go again. But, guess what? My old friend General Shields had me released. Suddenly, I found I was famous. What a delightful turn of events. I was described in Northern newspapers as "notorious" and by the sobriquet that was to stick, *"La Belle Rebelle."* One account even claimed that I had helped Jackson by *"playing Delilah to General Banks"* dancing before him at a ball, and draping *"a large and elegant secesh flag over my admirer."* I found myself to be idolized by the men of the Southern armies while the soldiers of the Northern armies were quite captivated by me. I found all this attention to be quite gratifying.

However, things were about to take an unexpected turn. While I have always enjoyed the attentions of the men around me, I was never smitten by any of them. That is, until I met C.W.D. Smitley, a paroled Southern officer waiting for a pass to rejoin his outfit. I allowed him to walk me home from a party one evening. We said a long, lingering good night in the moonlight. I decided to trust him and asked him if he would carry a message to General Jackson and he agreed to do so. My maid, Eliza, cautioned me that she had seen this man being friendly with the Yankees. But, I was in love and wouldn't believe that my paramour could be a spy. Bluntly, I asked him if he was a Northern agent. He said he was not. I continued to worry however, and the next day went to the boarding house where he was lodged and demanded that he tell me the truth. He emphatically denied being a northern spy. Unhappily for me, he turned out to be a scout for the 5th West Virginia Cavalry. He promptly reported my secret communique to his superiors who in turn, communicated with Secretary of War Stanton. Stanton took immediate action. I was arrested – again.

The Union officers came into my home and my family and I were lined up against a wall. The soldiers searched the house and found incriminating papers I had hidden in the desk. I was led away through a crowd of people, some of whom came to sympathize and others to jeer. I cried all the way to Washington. For the first time, I was in a really tight spot and no amount of flirting or bravado would get me out of it.

I was locked in a prison cell. From its windows, I could see Pennsylvania Avenue and the house where just a short time before, I had made my debut. I have never felt so frightened or so alone. I was confronted by Superintendent Wood, my jailer, and Lafayette Baker, the Director of Federal Detectives. *"Aint you pretty tired of your prison aready? I've come to get you to make a free confession now of what you've did agin our cause."* With a cockiness I didn't really feel, I contemptuously replied, *"When you've informed me on what grounds I've been arrested and given me a copy of the charges, I'll make a statemen*t." Baker offered that I take an oath of allegiance that he could take to Secretary Stanton. I replied, *"Tell Mr. Stanton for me, I hope when I commence that oath, my tongue may cleave to the roof of my mouth. If I ever sign one line to show allegiance, I hope my arm falls paralyzed to my side."* I then brazenly ordered Baker out of my cell telling him, *"I'm so disgusted I can't endure your presence any longer."*

At these words, to my everlasting surprise, cries of *"Bravo"* echoed through the prison. It seems my fellow prisoners had been listening to the exchange of words. Their encouragement made me feel ever so much better. That evening, I heard a cough and a small object rolled across the floor of my cell. It was a nutshell with a Confederate flag painted on it and inside was a note of sympathy. Even here in Yankee land, I had my supporters. I passed my days in prison peacefully enough, reading *Harpers*, eating peaches and singing. The sound of my voice happily singing songs of defiance to the North was enjoyed by both my fellow prisoners and by our guards. When I was allowed to walk in the narrow exercise yard, I conducted myself in a queenly manner with grace and dignity.

I might at this point tell about my prison courtship by Lieutenant McVey. We had been acquainted many years earlier but had not seen each other for a long time. The handsome Lieutenant had been badly injured in battle and left for dead by his southern comrades. When the Union army moved in, the soldiers placed him in a basket for corpses. Then, to the surprise of all present, the Lieutenant moved. He was brought to Washington to recover from his injuries, and fortunately was incarcerated in a cell just across the hall from my own. Needless to say, we resumed our friendship and whenever permitted, would sit together in the yard. Well, one thing led to another, and we soon announced our engagement. We planned to marry as soon as we gained our freedom and I was as happy as an imprisoned, newly engaged, eighteen-year-old could possibly be. Planning our wedding, I asked permission to buy my trousseau in Washington, but that nasty old War Department coldly denied my request.

The long confinement and the stifling heat began to wear me down. A picture of Confederacy President, Jefferson Davis had been smuggled in to me which I promptly hung in my cell. As punishment, I was confined to my cell for many long summer months. Due to the lack of fresh air, exercise, and stifling heat, I became listless and thin, and eventually became ill with typhoid fever. At last however, there was good news. I and several others, were to be involved in a prisoner exchange. The only unfortunate element was that Lieutenant McVey was not to be a participant in the exchange.

After all I had been through, my departure from the prison was an unmitigated triumph. Looking through the carriage windows, I could see crowds of people as they pressed forward calling my name. When we reached Richmond, the Richmond Light Infantry Blues presented arms in my honor. I was a celebrity. In the following weeks, generals came to visit me. Women stopped me in the street to praise me. Invited by General Jackson to review the troops, I sat on my horse, proudly wearing a very smart gray "honorary captain" of the Confederacy riding costume. The months passed by happily although poor Lieutenant McVey was still imprisoned. And so, as time went on, I lost interest in him.

I returned home to Martinsburg. The Federals were very unhappy to have me within Union lines as I was considered a serious liability. Secretary Stanton ordered my arrest; again. I was taken to Carroll Prison in Baltimore where I flew Confederate flags from my cell window and gaily sang the defiant lyrics of "*Maryland, my Maryland.*"

She is not dead, nor deaf, nor dumb
Huzza! She spurns the Northern scum!
She breathes! She burns! She'll come! She'll come!
Maryland! My Maryland!

One evening, I found an arrow on the floor of my cell with a note attached. The message said that "C.H." wanted me to realize that I had many sympathizers and that he would be in the square opposite on Thursdays and Saturdays. The note said he would attempt to communicate with me by shooting rubber balls into my cell with a bow and arrow. I was to cut open the balls, put my messages inside, sew them up again, and toss the balls out the window as energetically as I could. I liked this conspiracy and was happy to comply with the instructions. In this way, we carried on a lively and very successful correspondence passing clippings and confidential notes about the Union army. Unfortunately, again the heat and close confinement left me very ill. As a humanitarian gesture, I was again sent to Richmond but with a sharp warning that should I show myself again inside Federal lines, I would be in the worst trouble of my life.

The following months were a very difficult time for me. My dear father died and I suffered recurrent bouts of illness. Doctors recommended that I go on a long sea voyage to recuperate. To me, the recommendation meant an opportunity to again serve the South. Once more, I would be a courier and this time would carry letters from President Jefferson Davis to the British government. In May, 1864, I set sail on the blockade runner, *Greyhound.* Everyone aboard hoped to make the Atlantic crossing avoiding notice of the Federal gunboats. It was not to be. We were spotted and fired on by the northern gunboat, *USS Connecticut.* The *Greyhound* was boarded by a group of sailors led by a young, handsome lieutenant named Samuel Hardinge. At once, I was smitten hard by the way "*his dark brown hair hung down his shoulders, his eyes were large and bright...My Southern proclivities strong as they were, yielded for a moment to the impulses of my heart.*" The handsome young man immediately returned my affection. In the weeks following, as we sailed back to North America, we both realized we were deeply in love. Although I was his prisoner, it was not long before he asked me to marry him and we were plotting various ways for me to escape. With his help, when the voyage ended, I was able to flee to Canada and from there to England. My days as a Confederate spy had come to an end.

EPILOGUE

For aiding and abetting an enemy agent, Samuel Hardinge was arrested, tried and dismissed from the Navy for neglect of duty. From Canada, Belle fled to Liverpool where the lovers were eventually reunited. They married and the always persuasive Belle managed to turn her new husband into a spy for the South. While Belle remained in England, Hardinge returned to America this time as a courier for the South. He was arrested again as a Southern spy and died in prison.

Belle, pregnant and widowed was short of money. She wrote a two-volume memoir titled, *Belle Boyd in Camp and Prison* which told about her war experiences. She appeared on the London stage reading from her memoirs before large audiences. After the war, she went on to a theatrical career in both England and America. She was married twice more and at age fifty-seven and penniless, died of a heart attack while on a speaking tour in Wisconsin. Ironically, she is buried in Wisconsin, far from her beloved Virginia.

ELIZABETH BLACK

When I reflect on my seventy-one years, I regard my time with the American Red Cross during World War II as among my most satisfying and fulfilling years. It is both astounding and embarrassing to make that confession. How could those terrible years of horror and death be fulfilling? Before you judge me some sort of loathsome monster let me tell you a little about myself. My name is Elizabeth Black but I am called Betty by just about everyone. I was born in 1912, into a wonderful and supportive family in Pittsburgh, Pennsylvania. It was my good fortune to be endowed with an innate talent for drawing and painting and my indulgent parents encouraged me to study art at Carnegie Tech in Pittsburgh, and the prestigious Art Students League of New York.

In 1940, the new Carnegie Library in Pittsburgh opened and it led to my first big break as an artist. I was selected, from hundreds of applicants, to paint for the library, twenty-five life-sized portraits of some of the most famous American literary giants. I painted larger-than-life likenesses of Henry Wadsworth Longfellow, Nathanial Hawthorne, Henry David Thoreau, Mark Twain and other celebrated authors and poets. These portraits were permanently mounted in huge niches that lined the walls of the main reading room of the library, each niche carefully labeled with the famed writer's name. It took me over two years to complete the project. I worked mostly from photographs but there were no photos of Emily Dickenson available. My painting of her was done from her own self-description. It was hoped that the portraits would inspire the library's patrons to read the best of American literature. I was just twenty-eight years old and with the success of the portraits, my reputation as an artist was made. I was a successful woman artist in an art world dominated by men. My career soared even higher as wealthy Pittsburgh families, such as the Mellons, Craigs and Shaws and members of Pittsburgh society's Junior League commissioned me to paint portraits of their children as they "came of age." I was on my way to what I was certain would be a long and successful career.

However, things did not work out the way I thought they would. World War II intervened and I felt compelled to do something to support the American war effort. In those days, women helped mainly on the home front as volunteer bandage-rollers, nurses in hospitals or as factory workers, a là Rosie the Riveter. I wanted to find another way to be of service. In 1943, I joined the American Red Cross and became part of the American Red Cross Clubmobile Service. The purpose of the clubmobiles was to bring a touch of home to the battle-weary and lonely American GIs throughout the war-torn countries of Europe. One hundred and seventy trucks were converted into clubmobiles and were driven and staffed by three Red Cross volunteers. Each clubmobile carried a donut machine and a primus stove used to heat water for making coffee which we prepared in 50-cup urns. The back of the bus held a lounge with built-in benches that could be converted into bunks. Every clubmobile was equipped with a Victrola, loud speakers and current phonograph records. Also on board were paperback books, cigarettes, candy and gum, all free for the servicemen. We traveled with the rear echelon of the Army corps and received our orders from the Army. The clubmobiles crisscrossed Europe and served the troops in England, France, Italy, Bulgaria, Luxembourg and Germany until the end of the war on May 7, 1945. Our job was to bring a bit of home to the weary and homesick GIs. Most of these soldiers and sailors were really just kids, teenagers or in their early twenties and away from home for the first time.

Not just any girl could be part of this select group. There were specific requirements that had to be met. We had to be between the ages of twenty-five and thirty-five, have some college and also some work experience. We had to be healthy, physically "hardy," sociable and attractive. The Red Cross called us Service Club Staff Assistants, but the GIs called us "Donut Dollies." It is said that we passed out four hundred donuts every minute; 1.6 billion during the course of the war. Along with the donuts, we distributed coffee and cigarettes, accompanied by dances, jokes and lively banter. We were not pin-up girls like Betty Grable or song-and-dance talents like Carmen Miranda but we could "talk" baseball and enjoyed jitterbugging to recorded Glenn Miller music such as "In the Mood." We were attractive, young, healthy American girls, and with a smattering of innocent and harmless flirting, reminded the lonely GIs of the sweethearts they left behind. We spent much of our time just listening to the boys talk about home, family, wives and girlfriends. In other words, we brought a small bit of "home" to the front lines. These courageous young men faced death every day and being able to talk to a pretty American girl from back home really meant a lot to them. It meant a lot to us too as we felt we were doing our part for the war effort by helping lift the morale of these brave young warriors.

We looked the part too. We wore special uniforms consisting of a white shirt, battle-dress styled jacket, trousers and a visored ARC (American Red Cross) cap. Our uniforms were made of RAF blue-gray wool. A Red Cross patch was sewn on the upper left sleeve. We wore special ID tags which included our name, service (ARC), blood type, 5-digit ARC serial number, religion, and date of tetanus vaccination. Yes, this was serious, deadly business and our mission was to do what we could to mitigate the horror with a cup of coffee and a friendly smile. I felt indeed fortunate to be one of the girls selected to be a "Donut Dolly." I trained for six weeks in Washington D.C. before boarding a ship bound for England. By now I was thirty-one years old and more than ready to do my part for the war effort. I found the work to be immensely rewarding, but must admit I was absolutely terrified by the relentless bombing of London during the "Blitz." The other girls and I were completely unprepared to be in a war zone. Sadly, fifty-two American Red Cross volunteers died during the war.

One day, I had a "Eureka" moment. I realized that by using my artistic talent, I could do something unique for the servicemen. Painstakingly, I wrote a seven page business plan on thin, onion skin paper and submitted it to the American Red Cross and the United States military. I carefully explained my idea and detailed how my plan could be realized. I described my artistic abilities and how my talent could be used to bolster the morale of the GIs. My plan was to draw charcoal sketches of the fighting men and send these sketches to their parents or wives back home. I explained that it was very important that a lottery be arranged to determine which servicemen would be sketched as it was impossible for everyone to sit for an artistic rendering. I explained that I would need supplies of paper and charcoal and that I would continue to travel with the clubmobile but would do portraits instead of passing out donuts. The drawings would be something special. Each selected soldier or sailor would "sit" for me and his sketch would be sent to the worried loved ones who were anxiously waiting for his safe return. *"Back of every soldier's willingness to sit for a drawing of himself is his desire to send it to someone back home. Thus, the faces of their boys, the flier, the gunner, the engineer, the paratrooper, the mechanic, records for the American people the story of the American Army in this war."*

To my delight, my plan was approved. During the next two years, I sketched about one thousand GIs in six different countries, sometimes completing as many as a dozen sketches in one day. The boys loved it and so did I. As the Allies pushed their way through Europe, I was there too with my paper, charcoal and journal. The so-called "model" would sit for me while his buddies gathered around and made good-natured teasing comments, and the ribbing would fly back and forth while I drew. I took my time with each sketch as I wanted to be sure to capture each soldier's expression. Although it was never mentioned, we all knew that some would never return home. In spite of this awareness, the drawing sessions were lighthearted and fun and provided a welcome respite for the war-weary young men. I asked each "model" to sign and date his sketch. I also asked each to sign my journal where they wrote their home address so the sketch could be mailed to their loved ones back home. Many also wrote in the journal wonderful heartfelt and poignant messages and poems to me. On October 21, 1944, a staff sergeant from Los Angeles wrote, *"My best wishes to the finest personality I have ever met and sincerely an artist to scetch (sic) a mug like mine. Thanks a million."* A poem written by a soldier from Brooklyn ended with, *"Never will I forget that friendly gal/Who made me smile, thank you pal."* Believe me when I tell you, I would not exchange my emotions after reading these entries, and others like them, for anything in the world.

I also received many letters from the GIs' worried mothers, wives, sisters and girlfriends telling me how much receiving the sketches in the mail meant to them. *"It's a nice gift, a really nice gift,"* wrote one family after receiving it. *"It looks just like him,"* wrote another. I heard from a mother who received the drawing about a year after her son had been deployed. He was sketched on leave in Holland after fighting in the Battle of the Bulge. One daughter wrote, *"I just cried my eyes out. I thought it was beautiful."* Sometimes, because of the slow wartime mail, the soldier had been killed by the time the sketch reached his family. Nevertheless, a family member would send a thank you letter to me, a stranger. One regiment I sketched was among the first to land in Normandy on December 6, 1944. Not many survived. *"Thank you so much. We will cherish this forever. He was killed a month ago."* I think now you understand why I called this emotional, heart wrenching time my most fulfilling and rewarding years.

I met my future husband, John Wesley Black, a Navy commander, in Cherbourg, France in 1944. Coincidentally, his surname also was Black. Later that year, we married in the American Cathedral in Paris. After the war ended in 1945, we sailed back to the United States and settled in Staunton, Virginia, not far from Charlottesville. Our little family grew with the birth of two sons. I diligently tried to resume my career but there was not much call for a portrait artist in the small town. It appeared that my job now, like almost all other American women, was to support my husband and raise my children, not establish myself in my own career. I had briefly told my sons about my wartime experiences but they really were not interested and hardly listened. But, it was an important part of who I was as a person that I didn't want to lose. When my husband and I settled in Virginia, I tenderly placed my clubmobile memorabilia into my husband's navy foot locker. Into the trunk went the journal that was signed and dated by each "model" along with their comments and poems. I had taken photographs of about one hundred of my sketches and these too went into the trunk. The appreciative notes and thank you letters I received from the servicemen's families all went into the trunk.

My husband suffered a heart attack and died in 1956. Several years later, with my sons now grown, I moved to California and later Oregon in the hopes that this area of the country would be more conducive to restarting my career, but it never happened. Although I barely mentioned the existence of the trunk and its contents to anyone, it was very important to me and as I moved from Virginia to California and finally to Oregon, the trunk went with me. Of course, it was very disappointing to not be able to re-establish my profession as a portrait artist, but it was my choice to exchange my budding career for my contribution to the war effort. The decision was all mine and I am proud of it.

EPILOGUE

When Elizabeth Black died in 1983 of a heart attack, the trunk ended up in the attic of her son George, who was living in California. There it remained untouched and unopened for thirty years. Somehow, it then made its way to the home of her son John in Germantown, Tennessee. One day in the spring of 2010, over seventy years after the end of the war, John opened the leather handled trunk and discovered his mother's treasure trove of memorabilia. Imagine his shock and surprise to learn of this significant part of his mother's life about which he was mostly unaware. He decided to follow-up to see if he could locate the GIs in the photos/sketches. He had some success but many of the "models" who were now in their eighties or nineties had already passed away. John contacted WQED in Pittsburgh who put together a wonderful video titled "*Portraits for the Homefront: The Story of Elizabeth Black.*" If any readers of this story are, or know of any soldier or sailor who was sketched by Elizabeth Black, please be aware that through social media, there is an interactive project titled "Finding Elizabeth's Soldiers." They would be very interested in hearing from you, as would this writer.

Sadly, it should also be noted, that Elizabeth Black's life-sized portraits of the literary giants for the "permanent" collection of the Carnegie Library were removed during the Library's renovation during the 1960's. Today, despite a diligent search, the whereabouts of the portraits remain unknown.

IN THE AIR AND ON THE GROUND

BESSIE COLEMAN

April 30, 1926 was a momentous day. At least it was for me. You see, that was the day I died. I was just 34 years old. But this little Negro girl from Texas had accomplished quite a lot in her short life. In case you're wondering, in those days, people of color weren't called blacks or African-Americans or any other popular sobriquet of today. The slogan "Black is Beautiful" later changed everything and became a source of pride for my race. But back then, many white people referred to people of my race with vile racist names that I won't repeat. Filled with self-respect, we proudly called ourselves Negroes; occasionally we said "colored" but I never was fond of that word.

I was always an ambitious type of kid. The tenth of thirteen children, I attended a segregated, one-room school where I excelled, especially in math. Life for me was a routine of school, church, chores and pickin' cotton. But, there was one thing of which I was certain. I was going to "*amount to something.*" After graduating from high school, I enrolled in the Oklahoma Colored Agricultural & Normal University but after just one semester, ran out of money and returned home to Texas.

OK girl. So watcha gonna do now? My brothers were living in Chicago and I went off to live with them. I got myself a job as a manicurist at the White Sox Barber Shop and my life took a dramatic turn. Many of the shop's customers were Negro soldiers returning on leave from World War I. Let me tell you those "doughboys" could really tell some stories. These men were brave and adventurous and exciting and thrived on danger. What captivated me especially were their stories about flying. I was hooked. I had always had an interest in aviation and now I wanted to fly more than anything. I tried enrolling in flight school but no school would take me on. Why? Because I was a woman and I was a Negro. A double whammy! Even Negro aviators refused to train me. My brothers teased, *"Bessie, it's too bad you're not French. Those French Mademoiselles are piloting planes in the war."*

One of the regular customers in the barber shop was Robert S. Abbott, founder and publisher of the *Chicago Defender*, the foremost Negro newspaper in the country. He said, *"Bessie, learn French and get yourself to aviation school. The Defender will help sponsor you if you can find some additional sponsors."*

Well, that sure sounded like a plan to me. I found myself some other sponsors, notably Jesse Binga. Mr. Binga was the first Negro man to own a Chicago bank. He arrived in Chicago from Detroit with just ten dollars in his pocket. Starting out as a bootblack, he rose to become the founder and president of the Binga State Bank. My next step was to quit the barber shop and I got a job managing a chili restaurant. I also enrolled in the Berlitz School to learn the old "parley-vous francais." Before long, I could speak French passably well, and in 1920, I actually went to Paris and enrolled in flight school. I learned to fly a Nieuport Type #2 biplane. The plane had "*a steering system that consisted of a vertical stick the thickness of a baseball bat in front of the pilot and a rudder bar under the pilot's feet."*

1921 was, for me, a year of a very proud and singular accomplishment. I became the first Negro woman to earn an international aviation license from the Federation Aeronautique Internationale and the first American of any ethnicity or either gender to do so. When I returned to the United States I was a media sensation. Can you believe it? This little 'colored girl' from Texas, a phenomenon!

Now that I had my pilot's license I still needed a way to earn a living. Commercial aviation would not come into existence for about another ten years and even so, no one would hire a woman pilot. I quickly realized that if I wanted to fly, I would need to become a barnstormer and perform for paying audiences. Barnstormers were a special fearless group of people addicted to adventure, always ready to push their flimsy aircraft to the limit with dangerous acrobatic maneuvers. I returned to Europe for additional training and before long, was back in the U.S. performing daredevil tricks such as figure eights, loops and near- ground digs for American audiences. The press dubbed me "Queen Bess" and I was very popular with both Negroes and whites.

Barnstorming was a perfect fit for me. When I was performing I felt exhilarated. I felt free. It actually was the only time I felt really free – free as the air - free as anyone else – free from Jim Crow laws – free to be me. I could fly, earn money, become something of a celebrity and make my way in the male dominated world of aviation. Most women barnstormers were wing-walkers. But, I was something special. I had my pilot's license and audiences loved to see me, a Negro woman at the controls of a plane. And I ate it up.

It didn't take me long to realize that to succeed in this business meant a healthy mix of technical aerial proficiency, show business and self-promotion. I quickly learned to dress the part and wore jodhpurs, quasi-military garb, a long, white silk scarf, a flying helmet and goggles. Man, I looked good! I eagerly went along with all of it, telling the press truths, half-truths and occasionally, full-out untruths about my flying career. My sponsors and my cheering fans were very enthusiastic. Of course, not everyone liked me. I was called a "show-off," a publicity hound, temperamental, an exaggerator and other names of that ilk, but "Queen Bess" was popular with most folks.

In 1922, I appeared at an event honoring veterans of the 369th Infantry Regiment of World War I. I was billed as *"the greatest woman flier"* and the show featured aerial displays by myself and eight other American ace pilots and a Negro parachutist at Curtiss Field in Long Island, New York. The crowd loved the show. I was well on my way to fulfilling my childhood ambition to *"amount to something."*

An added bonus, my stunts popularized aviation in the Negro community and this was the second part of my dream: to establish a school for young Negro aviators. I was very proud of my accomplishments as an aviation pioneer and I hoped my personal story would serve as an inspiration to other Negro men and especially Negro women, to not be afraid to dream. I was frequently invited to lecture and I would remind the audience that although we live in a time of racial prejudice and segregation, we can overcome these barriers if we let ourselves dare to dream. The establishment of an aviation school for African-Americans would help shrink that barrier.

Unfortunately, I would not live to see it happen. On April 30, 1926, my mechanic and publicity agent, William Wills and I were making a reconnaissance flight over a field in Jacksonville, Florida. I was scheduled to perform the following day in an air show sponsored by the Negro Welfare League of Jacksonville. I had recently purchased a used Army Curtiss JN-4 (Jenny). I knew the old "has-been" biplane was in fragile condition but it was all I could afford. I wanted to take a test flight to get an aerial view of the field before the show. Will was flying the biplane seated in the front pilot's seat while I was seated in the passenger seat behind him. I'm kind of short so I didn't bother buckling up my seat belt because I wanted to be able to lean over the side of the plane to study the geography of the field where I would be performing the next day. As the creaky biplane lifted into the air, the by-now familiar sense of exhilaration, excitement and freedom swept over me. Will flew the "Jenny" to two thousand feet and circled around the field a few times. I leaned over the side making note of the field's terrain. Suddenly, the unreliable aircraft increased speed and gained altitude. I was overcome with a rapid succession of emotions. Surprise. Bewilderment. Anxiety. Fear. The plane abruptly fell into a nose-dive. My heart lurched up into my mouth while my stomach hovered somewhere near my feet. I screamed for Will to *"level her off"* but of course he couldn't hear me over the combined roar of the engine and the racing wind. One nauseating moment later, the old, open-cockpit, two-seater flipped over onto its back. I fell out. With Will doing his best to regain control of the plane, the "Jenny" crashed and burned.

EPILOGUE

When the wreckage was later examined, it was determined that a wrench used to service the engine had slid into the gear box, jammed it and was the cause of the deadly crash Despite her untimely death, Bessie's dream to "amount to something" came true. Every April 30th, African-American aviators, both men and women, fly in formation over Lincoln Cometary in southwest Chicago and drop flowers on her grave. Roads at O'Hare International Airport in Chicago and Frankfurt International Airport in Germany are named for her. In 2012, a bronze plaque with Bessie's likeness was installed on the front doors of Paxon School for Advanced Studies. The school is located on the Jacksonville, Florida site of Bessie's fatal flight

Following her death, black flyers founded the Bessie Coleman Aero Clubs. Black women pilots founded the Bessie Coleman Aviators Organization which is open to women pilots of all races. Her photograph hangs alongside other elite aviation pioneers in the Wright Brothers Visitor Center in Kitty Hawk, North Carolina. In 1995, The United States Postal Service issued a 32-cent stamp in her honor.

THE LADY OF COFITACHEQUI

Gold! Silver! Precious gems! The siren song of untold riches echoed across the vast Atlantic Ocean. The call was heard by Spanish explorer Hernando DeSoto and he and his followers set sail for the New World. The time was not quite mid-16th century. The conquistadors made their way through South America primarily focusing on Peru, plundering, pillaging, torturing and murdering in their insatiable quest for gold and silver. When DeSoto thought he had looted all the treasure that Peru had to offer, he set his sights on North America. His goal was to embark on a long land expedition through the southeastern portion of the continent in pursuit of the region's rumored fortune in gold and jewels.

This is where I make my entrance into the story. I am the Chief of the Cofitachequi Indians and well-known in the region as The Lady of Cofitachequi. We make our home in the area presently referred to as South Carolina. You're probably surprised that a woman is Chief of our tribe. That's the way it has always been among our people. Women run the show and do so very successfully, I might add. Our nearby neighbors all have traditional male chiefs, but we Cofitachequi are a proud people and have our own traditions. My tribesmen believe me to be a descendant of the Sun, a deity of great importance to our agricultural way of life. In short, I am a powerful woman who is honored, respected and beloved by my people. In fact, so well-loved, I am not required to walk anywhere. As a sign of the high esteem and respect in which I am held, my followers insist that I be carried on a litter covered with white linen wherever I wish to go. My followers are skilled farmers and crafters of beautiful pottery and we are quite an affluent tribe. You see, I have been raised by tribal chiefs and have been taught the myths and sacred powers that have enabled me to ensure that my people prospered. Of course, we are always wary of nearby rival chiefdoms and perpetually on the prowl for allies.

My encounter with Hernando DeSoto began on May 1, 1540. My lookouts reported that a large contingent of white men were gathered on the opposite side of the Savannah River. I had my bearers carry me on my litter down to the river to see them. They presented a fascinating and rather amusing sight. We saw men with white skins who were dressed most peculiarly. On their heads they wore huge helmets, some decorated with a feather. Hard metal vests covered their upper torsos, while their legs were enveloped in rather bulbous pants. Their feet were encased in heavy leather boots. They looked ridiculous! Their outfits were completely inappropriate for both the climate and our mix of agricultural and forest environment. I must admit my followers and I enjoyed a good laugh at their expense. In contrast, I had dressed both carefully and impressively in my best animal skins and wore lovely copper and pearl jewelry.

I climbed aboard my fine dugout canoe which was covered by an ornamental awning to protect me from the sun and outfitted with ample cushions to ensure my comfort. Accompanied by eight women, we rowed across the river to meet the strangers. Just as I intended, the Spaniards were impressed with this display of my authority and power. I did not believe that these white men possessed god-like capabilities but recognized that they were militarily very strong. It did not take me long to realize a peaceful encounter would be prudent. Courteously, I introduced myself to their leader whose name was Hernando DeSoto and offered him my assistance with their expedition. Through an interpreter, I offered them corn from our large storehouses and housing accommodations in our village and agreed to provide them with canoes to carry them across the river to our community. In a gesture of good faith, I ceremoniously removed a long rope of pearls from around my neck, each pearl as large as a walnut, and placed it over DeSoto's head. In exchange, he gave me a quite nice ruby ring. Thus, the contract was sealed! We had successfully formed an alliance with these Spaniards, although, to be fair, it is possible the newcomers may have been unaware that the exchange of gifts had cemented our partnership. As I mentioned earlier, forming an alliance against rival chiefdoms is always one of my primary goals.

So, the Spaniards moved into our village and immediately DeSoto began asking questions about our precious metals. He wanted to see samples of all our minerals. We presented beautiful copper objects, freshwater pearls, and chunks of mica for his inspection. However, that was not what he was after. Europeans do not become rich with copper and mica. DeSoto wanted gold.

After spending a few weeks with us living in our homes, eating our food and helping themselves to the minerals in our storehouses, DeSoto and his men became disenchanted with the caliber of riches we had to offer. He decided to move on and asked me about the locations of other nearby chiefdoms where treasure might be located. I gladly directed him toward some nearby rivals.

Then the unthinkable happened. I was subjected to the most demeaning humiliation. The ungrateful DeSoto ordered his men to kidnap me and make me their hostage. I was forced, against my will, to join the Spanish expedition in their search for precious metals in nearby settlements. My feelings of embarrassment, shame and rage were overwhelming. We set off for a neighboring village. As I was now a hostage, there would be no litter to carry me. There was not even a horse for me. I had to *WALK!* My humiliation was unbearable and I was determined to escape. After a few weeks, an advantageous moment presented itself. I falsely told my guard, "I must attend to my necessities" and accompanied by three of my slave women, calmly walked off into the woods. I just kept on walking and my captors, ignorant of Indian ways, searched briefly, but never did find me. I eventually made my way back to my village where my people greeted me with overwhelming joy. I resumed my position and duties as Chief and beloved Lady of Cofitachequi as if this whole unpleasant incident had never happened.

EPILOGUE

History records that the Conquistador continued his plundering, thieving journey through the southeast to what is now Texas. He and his men are credited with being the first Europeans to cross the Mississippi River.

Throughout the expedition, DeSoto encouraged the local natives to believe he was an immortal sun god in a ploy to gain their submission without conflict. In 1542, he succumbed to a fever and died on the banks of the Mississippi River. The location of his burial site has never been found. Some historians believe that during the night, his men hid his corpse in blankets weighted down with sand and sank it in the middle of the river. The men were fearful that if the Indians learned of the death of their leader, they would attack. Whether or not this is the true story of DeSoto's demise, no one really knows.

.

SUSAN BUTCHER

The view presented from my cabin window is of a totally white landscape that is stark, desolate, forbidding and yet, otherworldly beautiful. It is a mostly silent world except for the wind and the intermittent barking of the dogs. It is just the way I like it.

My name is Susan Butcher and I didn't always live in the wilderness. I was born in December, 1954 and lived with my parents and my sister Kate in Cambridge, Massachusetts, a close-in Boston suburb. My father, Charlie, was the head of the family's chemical products company. My mother, Agnes, was a psychiatric social worker. Both my parents believed that children should be taught to be independent and be free to develop their own talents.

Even at an early age, I didn't particularly like being around people. What I did like were animals and the outdoors. My first dog, Cabee, part Labrador retriever, was the most important thing in my life. I walked Cabee three times a day and as we walked I called out for other dogs to join us. It was not unusual to see me, accompanied by a pack of fifteen or twenty dogs, wending my way along the city streets of Cambridge. I considered the dogs to be my friends and as I watched and listened to them, I learned how dogs communicated. I learned how to recognize by a bark or a howl when a dog felt playful or afraid or in a bad mood.

Every summer my family vacationed at my grandmother's house in Maine. I felt so at home there. Cabee and I were free to roam the countryside away from the city and away from people. I dreamed of building a wooden boat and sailing around the world – alone.

When I was fifteen, Cabee died and my parents divorced. The family separation and loss of my best friend were very hard. To help me through this difficult time, my aunt gave me a Siberian husky named Maganak. A new passion entered my life as I became immensely interested in huskies and frequently attended sled dog races in nearby New Hampshire. I borrowed books from the library about sled dogs and began training Maganak. To Mother's dismay, I bought another husky to be a teammate for him. Mother and I usually got along very well but having two large dogs in the house was not to her liking. She sent me and the dogs to my grandmother's house in Maine where I could live away from the city, have my beloved dogs and finish high school. I tried applying to a ship-building school in Maine but they refused me admittance because of my gender.

Father remarried and moved to Boulder, Colorado when I was seventeen years old, and after graduation, my two dogs and I went to Boulder. As a surprise, my step-mother ordered a dog sled for me from a nearby racing kennel. What a fantastic and thoughtful gift. I got a job at the kennel where my duties included helping train and run the dogs. Now, instead of having just two dogs, I was partly responsible for the care and training of fifty. I enrolled at Colorado State University for veterinary classes and was hired as a veterinary assistant. I learned how to give shots, take temperatures, check heartbeats, locate fractures and ease pain for a large variety of animals. The knowledge and experience I gained was to prove invaluable in the future.

It wasn't long afterward that I read a magazine article about the Iditarod race in Alaska which captured my imagination. The article told the story of the 1925 calamity that hit the former gold- rush town of Nome. Nome is located on the isolated northwest coast of Alaska. Its sole connection to the rest of the world was provided by the mushers who brought mail and supplies once a month from Seward, an ice-free seaport in southern Alaska.

In 1925, the "Black Death" also known as diphtheria, critically sickened two children in Nome. The symptoms of diphtheria are a sore throat and fever, followed by rapid heartbeat, difficulty breathing and ultimately, death. At the time, Nome had only one doctor, Curtis Welch. The disease spread quickly putting fifteen hundred Nome residents at risk. Dr. Welch believed that the best way to treat his patients was for each to remain isolated at home. In this way, he hoped to contain the disease. However, the only way to eradicate diphtheria is by vaccination.

Doctor Welch sent out an emergency message on the wireless to hospitals and clinics in Alaska asking for serum. The hospital in Anchorage, one thousand miles away, had three hundred thousand units of serum, but it was the middle of winter. How could the serum be shipped? The Bering Sea was frozen and no ship could get through until the spring thaw. There were two small single engine biplanes but they had been dismantled and stored for the winter. It was decided that the only feasible course was a sled dog drive along the mail and supply routes through Alaska's frozen, barren, and dangerous interior.

The doctors in the hospital in Anchorage carefully wrapped the vials of serum in several layers of quilting and canvas for protection against breakage and the fierce cold. Twenty volunteer drivers or mushers and one hundred and fifty fast dogs would make the frigid, perilous thousand mile trip. As time was of the essence, the teams formed relays to keep needed rest time to a minimum. The mushers and dogs faced temperatures of fifty below zero degrees. They went over ice-covered slopes and valleys and made their way through a blizzard in a relay that took five days and seven and a half hours to complete - a journey that ordinarily took twenty-five days. Dr. Welch vaccinated everyone in the town and within three weeks the residents of Nome were safe.

The Iditarod is an annual dog-sled race commemorating that life-saving relay. The race was conceived by a musher named Joe Reddington and the first Iditarod took place in 1973. It is considered the toughest race in the world. The mushers and dogs competing face one hundred mile per hour winds, blinding snow and whiteouts, thin ice, wild animals and temperatures that sometimes dip to seventy degrees below zero. The race begins in early March in Anchorage and concludes over a thousand miles away in Nome.

By 1975, I was twenty-one years old and had saved enough money working at the kennel to go to Alaska. I got a job in Fairbanks helping to save the endangered musk-ox. I also bought three Alaskan huskies. In summers, I worked in a salmon factory and enjoyed the work cutting up fish. I lived in the back of an old Volkswagen or sometimes in a tent. I didn't spend much time with the other factory workers as I really don't care much for talking. I like to work.

In 1977, I convinced a bush pilot to drop me and my dogs into the wilderness of the southern Wrangell Mountains near the Canadian border. The location was very much to my liking and became my home base for several years. The only way in or out was by plane or snowshoes. The closest civilization was fifty miles away. I had my gun and a supply of rations for me and the dogs – beans, rice, flour and lots and lots of peanut butter. I shot and killed moose, caribou, sheep and small animals during the hunting season. I chopped firewood and built a small cabin. It would sometimes be months before I saw another human. I immersed myself in the adventure of it all and most especially in the solitude.

I had been fascinated with the idea of entering the Iditarod for quite some time. Its bare bones approach to racing appealed to me. The basic philosophy of the race is to embrace stamina and self-reliance on the part of the mushers and to take pride in the meticulous care of the dogs. I thought with time and practice, eventually I could win the race. I was physically fit, five foot six inches tall, athletic, focused and determined. I realized that in order to win the trophy, I first must do my homework and that meant starting with the dogs. I learned how to control the dogs' high spirits and eagerness. I watched them carefully for signs of dehydration or sprains. I trained them to take my commands. Traditionally, the word "mush" was the signal for the dogs to go. I thought the sound too soft and preferred to say "Hike" as the signal for them to go. "Gee" meant turn right and "Haw" meant turn left; "Whoa" meant stop.

In order to find which dog would be the best leader, I methodically watched and learned the strengths and weaknesses of each dog. The "lead" dog must be intelligent, willing and confident. This dog is the brains of the team. Behind the lead dog are the "swing" dogs. Their job is to keep the team and the sled on the trail at the corners and help navigate the turns. The "wheel" dogs are positioned directly in front of the sled and are exceptionally strong and steady. They are the first to feel the pull of the sled as it breaks loose of the snow. The "team" dogs are between the "swing" and "wheel" dogs. They are chosen for their strength and endurance. The number of team dogs vary and the distance from the sled to the lead dog can be as much as forty feet. No reins are used and the musher controls the team by voice commands only.

I also had to train myself to be competitive for the grueling race. I had to build up my stamina and endurance. I was my own coach. Like all athletes, I learned to focus on my goal, which in my case, was to win a race that requires two weeks of concentration and effort. By 1978, I felt that the dogs and I were ready to compete. We had practiced over and over, run over the trails, experienced many misadventures, had come close to dying several times, but both the dogs and I had learned our lessons well.

Not just anyone can sign-up willy-nilly to compete. There are specific mandatory rules required by the Iditarod Trail Committee which must be strictly followed. In this race, the survival of mushers and dogs is on the line. Mushers must start out with at least twelve dogs and finish with at least six dogs on the towline. Injured or sick dogs may not be replaced. Mushers are required to carry a veterinary notebook in which each dog's condition is recorded. To protect the dogs' paws on the icy trails, mushers carry thousands of dog booties. The booties are sewn by hand and are made of polypropylene or fleece that dries quickly on the trail. An Iditarod veterinarian checks the health condition of each dog at checkpoints. The vet has the last word and there is no appeal. If the vet determines that a dog cannot continue, the dog is cared for at a checkpoint by a volunteer until the race is over and can be returned to its owner.

As required by the Trail Committee, each musher must carry the heavy survival equipment needed to meet nature head-on. In addition to food, water and cold-weather gear for the musher and the dogs, every racer must carry snowshoes, an Arctic sleeping bag and a large axe. They also are required to carry a small stove, heating oil and a change of clothing. Most mushers also carry a gun.

There are twenty-five checkpoints along the trail, one of which is the former boom town of Iditarod for which the race is named. Iditarod is a Native American word which means "distant place." At each checkpoint, mushers must show race officials that the sled carries the mandatory survival equipment. Racers are required to take one twenty-four hour rest stop at a checkpoint of their choice to rest the dogs. In addition, they must also take an eight hour rest at White Mountain, the second to last checkpoint before the final sprint to Nome.

In 1978, I decided it was time for me to put the dogs and myself to the test and entered the race for the first time. At eight o'clock on the morning of the race, I tied on my numbered white vest which all racers must wear. The vets examined each of my dogs to ascertain that they were healthy and fit. They then marked each dog with a dab of paint to prevent exchanges during the race. Sometimes a dog shook its head scattering paint on nearby spectators. I lined up with the other racers so we would be ready to leave at the required two-minute intervals. The dogs were very excited, leaping in the air and jumping sideways, eager to get moving. They were accustomed to being in the wilderness and were quite distracted by the hustle and bustle of Anchorage. Finally, at nine o'clock, the Race Marshall cut the ribbon, blew his whistle, and number one sled took off. After the two-minute interval, number two sled was off and so on until each of the forty to sixty competing sleds had received the starting signal.

I chose Tekla to be my lead dog. We understood each other very well and were able to learn from one other as we traversed the snow-covered trails. We were traveling along the bank of a river with the dogs running very fast. We approached a left turn and I called out "haw." Tekla refused to follow my command something she had never done before. Instead the dog turned right and left the trail with the rest of the dogs, the sled and me following behind. Just as we did so, the snow-covered trail collapsed into the river. Had Tekla not turned away, we all would have fallen into the icy water and probably perished. We finished the race in nineteenth place, the first time a woman finished in the top twenty.

From that time on, I raced every year and was considered a regular in the Iditarod lineup. Every race brought new adventures and some life-threatening misadventures. But I learned and the dogs learned and we kept improving. We continued to move steadily up the ladder to ninth place, then fifth place and finally to second place. This was also the year

I met David Monson. David was an attorney who sold dog food part time. He came to Alaska looking for freedom, outdoor living and to race sled dogs. We hit it off immediately and became very good friends.

When 1985 rolled around, I was confident that this was the year I would win the race. The dogs and I were by now an experienced and strong team and had a thorough knowledge of the race trails. I was in top physical shape. Most of the dogs had been raised and trained by me and were in topnotch racing condition. I chose Granite to be my lead dog. At first things went very smoothly, the dogs and I well in tune with one another. As night fell, we were far ahead of the sixty other teams – and then, disaster. I was driving seventeen dogs which meant the distance from Granite to my sled was forty feet. As I drove the dogs up the slope toward Rabbit Hill, I saw the ears of the lead dogs go up. When I reached the top of the hill I saw a huge pregnant moose next to the trail. I immediately threw over the sled to stop the dogs but I was too late. The moose, crazed with hunger, charged into the middle of the team, stomping and kicking the dogs. I grabbed my ax and ran to help them, shouting and waving the ax at the moose. I tried poking the huge beast but nothing helped. The dogs were in harness and could not get away from the berserk animal. The onslaught continued for twenty minutes. Granite bravely went after the moose but the moose grabbed the dog and slammed him into a tree.

At last, another musher arrived and shot and killed the crazed animal but the toll on the team was terrible. One dog was dead and another lay dying. In total, thirteen of the seventeen dogs had been badly injured. Of course, I had to withdraw from the race but as disappointing as it was to withdraw, it was nothing compared to the anguish I felt for the suffering of my four-legged friends. I flew with them to the veterinary hospital in Anchorage and slept on the floor to be near them while they recovered from their injuries. The race, continuing without me and my team, was won by Libby Riddles who, instead of me, became the first woman to win the Iditarod.

As badly as 1985 started, it did have a happy ending. David Monson and I were married in the dog yard at my home in Eureka, located one hundred miles south of the Arctic Circle. A musher friend named Rick Swenson was my "bridesmaid." Granite and Tekla were the ring bearers.

I spent most of the following year rebuilding my team for the 1986 race and by March we were ready to race and to win. You see, "*I do not know the word 'quit'. Either I never did or I have abolished it.*" Just like the previous year's race, we started out well. As we reached the river at Rainy Pass, two of the dogs fell through the surface ice and were stranded on a second shelf of ice several feet below. A second shelf of ice is sometimes formed as the weather alternately warms and cools creating a second layer of ice. The hole in the ice made by the dogs was too tight for me to be able to pull them straight up and out. I needed to get the ax. I spoke quietly and soothingly to the other dogs. I needed them to stay still for if they moved forward, both the dogs and the sled would fall through the ice and the dogs would be killed. I returned to the sled, got the ax and cautiously chopped away at the edges of the hole. With the hole now enlarged, I called to the two stranded dogs and as they scrambled upward, I carefully pulled them to safety.

We continued on for several days alternating between running and resting. I frequently stopped to wipe the dogs' frozen eyelashes and to pat and talk to them encouragingly. We were moving well and soon began to make up for the lost time and overtake the other teams. By the tenth day, I was in the lead with my "bridesmaid" Rick Swenson, just a few hours behind. Eventually, Rick caught up and we then began trading the lead back and forth. By now we were getting only a few hours of sleep each day and exhaustion was taking its toll.

The next day, after just eleven days on the trail, I was the first to cross the Burled Arch Finish Line in Nome in the record-breaking time of eleven days, fifteen hours and six minutes. The whole town ran out into the street to greet me. Bells rang, sirens screeched and everyone cheered. I was exhausted, numb and euphoric all at the same time. I did it! I had won the Iditarod!

At the banquet that night, I received the Joe Reddinton Trophy, fifty thousand dollars, and along with the other finishers, a belt buckle to show I had completed "The Last Great Race." In the spirit of the Iditarod, the tradition of the Red Lantern Award was presented to the last place team. Each year as the race begins, lanterns are lit and are not extinguished until the last dog has crossed the finish line.

I won again the following year and yet again the year after that, the first time anyone, man or woman, had won the race in three consecutive years. To put the icing on the cake, I won again in 1990 making me a four-time winner, the first woman to have won the Iditarod four times and the only person to win four out of five sequential years.

EPILOGUE

Susan Butcher retired from sled-dog racing in 1995 as she and David wanted to start a family. She planned on racing again in 2003 but as so often happens, fate stepped in and her plans went awry. It was discovered by her doctors that Susan was suffering from a blood disorder and she had to withdraw from the race. In 2005 she was diagnosed with acute myelogenous leukemia. Susan Butcher died in 2006 leaving behind her husband David and two daughters, Tekla and Chisana. She was fifty-one years old.

Her family was not all that was left behind; she also left her legacy. To followers of sled-dog racing, her name is synonymous with the Iditarod as she dominated the sport for over a decade. She competed in the Iditarod eighteen times and won four times. She placed with the top five finishers twelve times and was considered the 'best competitive dog sled racer in the universe." In 1979, she helped drive the first sled dog team to the twenty thousand, three hundred and twenty foot summit of Mount McKinley, (now Denali) the highest peak in North America. Susan was an animal lover and business woman as well as an advocate for wildlife and the environment. She was passionate about educating the public about the proper care of animals. She made good use of her celebrity status by visiting hospitals and speaking on behalf of the American Cancer Society's anti-smoking campaign.

Susan Butcher was awarded the Women's Sports Foundation Professional Athlete of the Year Award in 1987 and 1998. She was selected by *Sports Illustrated* as one of the "100 Greatest Female Athletes." In 2008, Governor Sarah Palin of Alaska honored her by establishing Susan Butcher Day which is annually observed the first Saturday of March. That same year, the University of Alaska announced the creation of the Susan Butcher Institute to develop public service and leadership skills among young Alaskans.

EMMA "GRANDMA" GATEWOOD

If you'll go with me to the mountains
And sleep on the leaf carpeted floor
And enjoy the bigness of nature
And the beauty of all out-of-doors,
You will find your troubles all fading
And feel the Creator was not man
That made lovely mountains and forests
Which only a Supreme Power can.

Emma Gatewood

Folks here in southern Ohio usually refer to me as a stubborn, hard-nosed woman and I guess they're pretty much right. But then, mule-headedness is a trait that is not unfamiliar to farm people. My name is Emma Gatewood and I was born October 25, 1887 in a log cabin along Raccoon Creek in southwestern Ohio. There were fifteen children in my family and I was the eighth born. Daddy lost a leg fighting in the Civil War and my family led a hardscrabble life, but still, we made out all right. I went to school in a one-room schoolhouse until the eighth grade and by then knew all I needed to know about farm life. I also knew my flowers and plants and which plants were for eating and which made good medicine. I could sew up a quilt and weave a rug. My days were spent mowing, gardening and digging up potatoes and I could handle most general chores as well as any man.

When I was nineteen, I married a smart, respected self-educated Renaissance man named P.C. Gatewood who also turned out to be a no-good drunk with a violent temper. He and I had eleven children. Besides doing all the cooking, cleaning and raising the kids, I worked right alongside the men in the fields. My husband and I were married for thirty years and that sorry excuse of a man beat me regularly. Finally, I mustered up my courage and left him. I got myself a divorce and the courts awarded me our farm and custody of the kids. With him out of my life, things got better. I've always enjoyed the outdoors and feeling close to nature as I do, I especially relished taking long walks and enjoying all of God's creation. It's a good thing that I took pleasure in a good walk as there was no other form of transportation available to me.

In 1949, while sitting in the waiting room in my doctor's office, I happened to come across a story in National Geographic Magazine that told about two fellas who had thru-hiked the then new Appalachian Trail. Wow! That caught my attention! The article explained that a thru-hiker hikes the entire Appalachian Trail from end to end in one season. I was sixty-two years old but *"knew immediately that this was something I had to do."* The article further said that a thru-hike on the Appalachian Trail

(A.T.) had never been done by a woman. Now that sounded like a challenge. *"I wanted the satisfaction of doing something I wanted to do, by myself. Just as I pleased. I couldn't swim. Couldn't drive a car. Didn't have money to travel by bus."* I thought, I could do this, after all, I have always been a good walker and have long wished to do something no woman has ever done.

The A.T. stretches from the southern Appalachians in Georgia to Maine's Katahdin Mountain. It is a two thousand one hundred and forty-seven mile trail that follows the ridgetops of fourteen states. It was explicitly designed to be hiked. The majority of the A.T. is forest or woodland but much of it is raw, extremely rugged terrain often over wide streams and steep, jagged mountains. Other portions of the Trail cross towns, roads and farms. Most thru-hikers begin at the small Visitors' Center at the base of Amicola Falls (Tumbling Waters) in Dawsonville, Georgia. From here, it is a steep eight mile climb to the actual start of the Trail at Springer Mountain and extends all the way to Katahdin Mountain in Maine. Hikers sign-in in huge register books at the Visitors' Center and many also share their comments. They note their "complaints and miseries, joys and sorrows, blisters, cold, hunger and thirst, panoramic views, good fellowship, bad weather, steep climbs, hard ground and aching bones" and why they appreciated the opportunity to hike the Trail. After a few days of hiking, A.T. "newbies" discard as much as thirty pounds of unnecessary items such as scuba gear and hard covered books.

By 1954, my kids were grown and I decided it was high time for me to tackle the A.T. My adventures, or I probably should say misadventures, began almost immediately. Instead of hiking south to north as most do, I took off for Maine, climbed Katahdin on the first day and started south. *"I got lost right off the bat."* Looking for water, I took a side trail and found a pretty, small lake. The water looked so enticing I decided to take a bath. It was lovely and when I emerged from the water, I immediately stepped on my glasses and broke one of the lenses. Dadgummit! I patched them as best I could with a Band-Aid but I could barely see. As if that wasn't bad enough, I found myself to be somewhat disoriented. Which way was it back to the Trail? I started walking in the direction I hoped was the right one. I was almost out of food and little black flies nearly drove me crazy biting my arms and legs and buzzing in and around my ears, eyes and mouth. No question about it – I was good and lost. Three days and two nights later, I at last came upon four rangers who had been searching for me. I told them, *"I wasn't lost. I was misplaced."* The rangers scolded me severely. *"Go home, Grandma."* I didn't know it at the time, but from that moment on, I would forever be known on the A.T. as Grandma Gatewood. With my tail between my legs, I did as I was told. I went home.

Undaunted by this disappointing setback, I set off again in May of the following year determined that this time I would be successful. I was now sixty-seven years old but no little trail was going to defeat a strong-willed woman like me. This time my plan was to walk from south to north. I figured that by the time I got to Maine the weather would be cold and *"the blackflies would freeze their tails off."* I told my family, *"I'm going for a walk in the woods."* They didn't hear from me again until six weeks had gone by and I had "walked" eight hundred miles. You see, after my little difficulty the previous year, I knew they wouldn't approve if I told them I was going to hike the entire Appalachian Trail from end to end. *Alone!* I made myself an over-the–shoulder sling out of a piece of denim and filled it with an old Army blanket, a plastic shower curtain I could use for shelter, a raincoat, one change of clothing, a cup, a first-aid kit, a little dried beef, some nuts, and a couple of tins of Vienna sausages. Altogether it was a load of about seventeen pounds. I laced up my high-top canvas Keds and I was off. Later, I was to be called a pioneer of ultra-light backpacking.

There weren't many long-distance hikers on the Trail then. Mostly it was day hikers who would hike one section at a time, go home and hike a different section another day, or another season or another year. Thru-hikers are those who hike the entire twenty-two hundred miles in one season and it generally takes about five or six months to complete. Of course there are exceptions, but most thru-hikers are young white men in their twenties or thirties, physically fit introverts who have a strong affinity for nature. Many hikers are people in transition - just out of school or recently retired, especially from the military. Some are between jobs or between marriages. There are two hundred and fifty shelters and campsites along the A.T. Most shelters are open three-walled structures with a wooden floor, spaced about a day's hike apart, close to a water source and a privy. A few are larger with full-service lodging with meals and composting toilets. In one of the large shelters, you might find yourself bunking with people from all walks of life - a retired Admiral, a recent college graduate, a corporation executive, a vacationing cop, or a young man trying to "find himself." A grandmother, hiking alone, is certainly unique and unexpected.

The A.T. crosses many roads so hikers can hitchhike into town for food and supplies. It has been described as a "society in motion" with its own set of rituals. It is permeated with a mystical fellowship that hikers refer to as "trail magic" – that is, assistance from strangers by random acts of kindness. A hiker might find a box of food and bottles of water that had been left for them on the trail. Sometimes a stranger will cook and offer food or lodging for the night. Offers of an opportunity to shower are greatly appreciated as are gifts and all encouragement. Sometime during the 1980's it became popular to assume a "trail name." Many names are very colorful and often are associated with a story that is connected to an individual hiker. Stories are told about Dan "Wingfoot" Bruce, Robie "Jumpstart" Hensley and Noel "The Singing Horseman" DeCavalante. The chronicles of "Grandma" Gatewood were destined to become part of the folklore.

Into this milieu of strapping young men and their backpacks came me, the "old lady" with the denim bag slung over one shoulder. To say they were surprised to see someone like me is an understatement. I had designed for myself a crown of sassafras leaves that drooped down over my ears to ward off flies, and with my age, my walking stick, my denim sling, my sassafras crown, my aloneness and singing hymns as I hiked along, I guess I made quite a picture. It wasn't long before Grandma Gatewood was a well-known figure on the Trail.

The nicest thing about my denim bag was that I didn't have to keep unstrapping it when I needed to jump across a wide crevice or climb over huge rocks on the mountain sides. On steep places I could pull up or lower the sack with fifteen feet of nylon rope or drag it behind me if I had to crawl. My Keds were very comfortable which was a good thing since my marble-sized bunions made wearing hiking boots painful. I don't have much use for tents and thought shelters might not be safe for a woman alone so I slept on or under picnic tables, on piles of leaves, and once under a van. I depended quite a bit on the generosity of others for shelter and food. They say I slept in more places than George Washington. That good old "trail magic." I knew my plants and herbs and could make myself a nice cup of tea or even my own medicine if I needed to. When I got hungry, I could make myself a nice salad of tender sassafras leaves and wild strawberries.

I had been on the A.T. for about seventeen days. There weren't many people and hiking was difficult. The Trail was unkempt and not well marked. One day, as I walked along, I heard an unfamiliar hissing sound. At first I thought it was some sort of bird but suddenly I felt something strike the leg of my pants. I looked down and saw a rattlesnake all coiled up ready to strike again. Terrified, I slammed down the point of my walking stick toward the rattler and as quickly as I could, jumped sideways out of striking distance. For an old woman, I could move fast if I needed to – and I needed to. That experience really shook me up and was one I hoped wouldn't be repeated.

As I hiked, I was continually awed by the beauty of nature – a crowd of pink wildflowers, a cascading waterfall, the scent of the pine forest, strange and wondrous bugs of all kinds, and curious, and occasionally unfriendly animals were my companions as I walked mile after mile.

I had been hiking for about two months when my secret was uncovered. Folks I met who were kind enough to give me shelter for the night were eager to hear about what I was doing. One thing led to another and pretty soon there were lots of people who were interested in my journey. A reporter from a local newspaper chased me down and pestered me to let him tell my story and take my picture. He thought a story about a hiking grandmother would be a compelling read and the publicity would do wonders for the A.T. I was reluctant at first. I just wanted to be left alone but finally relented. I sent my family a few postcards to let them know where I was so they didn't have to read about me first. Now they would know what I meant when I told them *"I was going for a walk."* After that, several other reporters tracked me down when word got around that I was seen near their town. They would ask their interminable questions and write their stories for the local newspaper. They asked me how I stayed warm on cold nights without a sleeping bag. Not a real problem. I would heat some flat rocks over a fire and lay down on them for warmth. That system worked very well. When I tramped through the woods near the Mason-Dixon Line, a brief AP dispatch about me appeared in hundreds of newspapers and therefore into hundreds of thousands of homes across the country. My story seemed to have captured the imagination of Americans everywhere. They all were interested in the sixty-seven year old grandmother hiking alone in tennis shoes from Georgia to Maine. I never did get what all the fuss was about.

Hiking through Pennsylvania was the most arduous so far. I was about at the half-way point and the most difficult part of the Trail was ahead of me. The A.T. led over jagged rocks that were remnants of the last Ice Age and I desperately needed new shoes. I had sliced open the sides of my tennis shoes to give my bunions more space but my feet were terribly swollen from all the walking. When I got to Palmerton, Pennsylvania I tried to stop at a hotel but they were so appalled by my bedraggled appearance they wouldn't let me stay. I found a fork at a campsite and did my best to comb my knotted–up, disheveled gray hair but I guess I presented quite a spectacle. When children saw me they sometimes shouted out, *"Look at the old lady tramp."* A clerk in a shoe store tried to find a pair of shoes that would fit me but even the largest size was much too small. My feet had simply swollen themselves out of women-sized shoes. He fitted me with a pair of men's size 8 1/2's which I found to be quite comfortable and gave me a little extra room if my feet continued expanding.

I crossed the Delaware River into New Jersey on July 22 and was stopped by a policeman who asked my name and said I had a phone call. Turned out to be a reporter for *Sports Illustrated.* She wanted to write a profile of the hiking grandmother and we made an appointment to meet in New York near the Hudson River Valley. I arrived about four hours late but she waited for me, asked lots of questions and wrote her story. I kept walking. Seems like folks in towns and hamlets everywhere had heard about me. People would come up to me with questions, some wanted autographs and others wanted to take my photo. I didn't mind, but I certainly was perplexed and astounded by all the attention. It was becoming such a routine that sometimes I wondered if I ever would make it to Maine. Near Holmes, New York I followed a side trail to the Ludington Girl Scout Camp and had dinner with the girls and their counselors. After dinner, we gathered around the campfire and I told the scouts story after story about my trip. In the three months I had been hiking, I had worn out three pairs of shoes and lost twenty-four pounds. I tried to keep to a pace of about seventeen miles a day, rain or shine, but some days I just couldn't do it.

By August 8, I was in Pittsfield, Massachusetts and it was raining. It had been raining on and off for the past several days. I didn't know it, but on that day, hurricane Connie reached its maximum intensity east of West Palm Beach, Florida. The hurricane was packing winds of one hundred thirty-five miles per hour and was forty miles wide. The National Weather Bureau issued small craft warnings from Block Island, Rhode Island to Cape Hatteras, North Carolina. Connie swept up the coast leaving death and destruction in her wake. The hurricane's winds slammed two freighters together near Hampton Roads, Virginia. Seventy Red Cross shelters in the Carolinas were crowded with fourteen thousand refugees. Six inches of rain dropped on New York City in twenty-four hours. I was two hundred miles north of the city and to say I was wet is an understatement. After slogging through the storm for hours, I finally found some shelter in an abandoned lodge. The door was off its hinges and the windows had been broken out. Rain poured through the holes in the roof and porcupines had eaten huge chunks out of the wooden floor. I made the best of the situation but I was feeling pretty miserable.

I hiked, or in reality, waded through Vermont's Green Mountain National Forest. The wind had abated somewhat and was now blowing at about forty miles per hour. The mountains were saturated with water and their streams were running wild, sending incredible amounts of water into the surrounding rivers. Many of the rivers were close to flood stage. Then, I got stuck. One of my regrets is that I never learned how to swim. Well, I was up against it now. Clarendon Gorge is forty feet from bank to bank and the water was gushing through the gorge at an incredible speed. I tried, but there was no way I could safely cross. I sat down and waited for hours for someone to come along and help me. Wouldn’t you know it but along came two nice Navy boys I had met a few days earlier on the Trail. One of the boys tied my bag onto his backpack with parachute rope. He tied one end of the rope around his waist and the other boy did the same with another length of rope. They looped the cord around my waist and with me standing between them, tied me firmly between the two making a “Grandma sandwich.” Each boy took hold of one my hands and we started across. The water reached our chests as we slowly made our way across the slippery stone riverbed. I couldn’t look. I tilted my head back and stared up at the sky and squeezed those boys’ hands as hard as I could. How did I ever let myself get in such a predicament? After about forty tension-filled minutes, we at last made it onto dry ground, thanks to the ingenuity of those two boys.

By now, I had hiked seventeen hundred miles with three hundred and fifty miles of the most isolated, perilous and difficult part of the Trail left to go. The White Mountains of New Hampshire and the intimidating 100-mile Wilderness of Maine lay ahead. The Wilderness is famous for its inaccessibility and isolation. I trudged on and was met with another unbelievable obstacle. Mother Nature wasn’t done with me yet. Just five days after hurricane Connie hit the coast, along came a second hurricane, this one named Diane. Although not nearly as ferocious or damaging as the earlier storm, Diane made herself known. The ground was still soaked from Connie and the rivers and streams were badly swollen and overflowing their banks. When Diane hit, many homes and businesses were destroyed. Bridges were washed away. Over two hundred people died from the combined storms. I kept on walking. I was now on my sixth pair of shoes.

The White Mountains are home to some of the worst and most unpredictable weather on earth. The continual winds are of gale-force velocity and it is not unusual for it to snow during the summer. The highest peak is Mount Washington, which at 6,288 feet is certainly not among the planet's highest elevation but due to the capricious extreme weather is among the most dangerous. Year-round temperatures average below freezing. The highest wind speed ever recorded, two hundred and thirty-one miles per hour, was recorded on this mountain. No one should attempt to reach its summit unprepared without proper clothing and emergency rations. I made it over but it was tough. Many before me had died due to hypothermia or falls, but I'm a tough old bird and outside of getting lost a few times and having to climb ladders with rungs set too far apart for me, I made it through all right.

At last I crossed the state line into Maine, a rugged and wild state. It was September and I had just about one hundred miles to go to reach Mount Katahdin, the end of the Appalachian Trail. My right knee had been bothering me the past few weeks and now was quite swollen. My pace had slowed to about eight miles a day. I approached the infamous 100-mile Wilderness, a wild country filled with rocks, boulders and lots and lots of stream crossings. I had again broken my glasses by stepping on them but had learned a lesson from my first attempt at the Trail and brought along a spare. Unfortunately, I lost one of the lenses of the spare and so could barely see. I kept going but a few days later, fell, twisted my ankle and broke what remained of my glasses. I walked on blindly over the last ten miles to Rainbow Lake and there before me was Katahdin.

The date was September 25, 1955 as I began my ascent of Katahdin Mountain. In twenty-six days I would celebrate my 68th birthday. I wore my seventh pair of sneakers. I had hiked two thousand and fifty miles through fourteen states from Georgia to Maine. By the time I wrote my name in the registry book at the end of the Trail, I had lost thirty pounds, my glasses were broken and my knee was painfully swollen. I didn't care. I stood at the summit of the beautiful and forbidding mountain and with my voice loud and proud, I belted out into the wind the first verse of America the Beautiful.

Oh Beautiful, for spacious skies,
For amber waves of grain
For purple mountain majesties
Above the fruited plain
America! America!
God shed His grace on thee
And crown thy good with brotherhood
From sea to shining sea.

I proudly said to myself, *"I did it. I said I'd do it and I've done it."*

There was one question that I was asked over and over by the helpful, sharing and kind folks I met on the Trail, by people who offered me shelter and food on the farms and in towns, and by reporters who pestered me for stories. That question was *"Why did you do it?"* I always replied, *"I thought it would be a lark. It wasn't."*

EPILOGUE

Grandma Gatewood was the first woman to thru-hike the Appalachian Trail alone. Six months before her 70th birthday, she returned to the A.T. and did it all again becoming the first person, man or woman, to hike the world's longest trail twice. In 1959, at the age of seventy-one, she hiked the two thousand mile Oregon Trail from Independence, Missouri to Portland, Oregon. In 1964, when she was seventy-seven years old, she completed hiking the A.T. for the third time by walking a five- hundred mile section of the Trail through New England.

A bust of Grandma Gatewood is in the Appalachian Trail Hall of Fame in Boiling Springs, Pennsylvania. She is credited with being a pioneer of women thru-hikers of the A.T. and of ultra-light minimalist hiking. She proved that hikers do not need fancy equipment, special training, guide books or need be a young male. All that is needed is the determination to keep putting one foot in front of the other, over and over and over. She inspired people to take an interest in nature and the environment and to take the time to appreciate the great outdoors. Her commitment to hiking brought much needed attention to the Appalachian Trail. That attention in turn, resulted in the formation of many local clubs which support the Trail's upkeep and maintenance. Her favorite trail, Old

Man’s Cave to Ash Cave in her home state of Ohio has been named Grandma Gatewood Memorial Trail. The hiking grandmother of twenty-four grandchildren, thirty great-grandchildren and one great-great grandchild continued to hike until her death in 1973 at the age of eighty-five.

BIBLIOGRAPHY

Marie Tharp

Burleigh, Robert, *Solving the Puzzle Under the Sea: Marie Tharp Maps the Ocean Floor,* Simon & Schuster Books for Young Readers, New York, New York, 2016

Felt, Hali, *Soundings: The Story of the Remarkable Woman Who Mapped the Ocean Floor,* Henry Holt and Company; New York, New York, 2012

Swaby, Rachel, *Headstrong: 52 Women Who Changed Science and the World,* Broadway Books, New York, New York, 2015

Grace Hopper

Beyer, Kurt W, *Grace Hopper and the Invention of the Information Age,* The MIT Press, 2009

Williams, Kathleen Broome, *Grace Hopper: Admiral of the Cyber Sea,* Naval Institute Press, Annapolis, Maryland, 2004

Laura Keene

Bogar, Thomas A., *Backstage at the Lincoln Assassination: The Untold Story of the Actors and Stagehands at Ford's Theater,* Regnery History, 2013.

Harbin, Billy J., *Laura Keene at the Lincoln Assassination,* The Johns Hopkins University Press. Baltimore, Maryland,

O'Reilly, Bill and Dugard, Martin, *Killing Lincoln,* Henry Holt & Co., New York, New York, 2011

Theodate Pope

Katz, Sandra L, *Dearest of Geniuses: A Life of Theodate Pope Riddle,* Tide-Mark, Windsor, Connecticut, 2003

Larson, Erik, *Dead Wake,* Crown Publishers, New York, 2015

Sybil Ludington

Amstel, Marsha, *Sybil Ludington's Midnight Ride,* Carolrhoda Books, Inc. Minneapolis, Minnesota, 2000

Berkin, Carol, *Revolutionary Mothers*, Alfred A. Knopf, New York, New York, 2005

Bibliography

Dacquino, V.T., *The Call to Arms*, Purple Mountain Press Ltd, Fleischmanns, New York, 2000

Winnick, Karen B, *Sybil's Night Ride*, Boyds Mills Press, Honesdale, Pennsylvania, 2000

Mary Katherine Goddard

Allen, Danielle, *Our Declaration: A Reading of the Declaration of Independence in Defense of Equality*, Liveright Publishing Corporation, New York, New York, 2014

Andrlik, Todd, *Reporting the Revolutionary War: Before There Was History it Was News*, Source Books, New York, New York, 2012

Schilpp, Madelon Golden and Murphy, Sharon M, *Great Women of the Press*, Southern Illinois University Press, Carbondale, Illinois, 1983

Belle Boyd

Abbott, Karen, *Liar, Temptress, Soldier, Spy,* HarperCollins, Publishers, New York, New York, 2014

Boyd, Belle, *Belle Boyd in Camp and in Prison,* originally published Blelick & Co, New York, 1805, Faust, Drew Gilpin, Forward, Louisiana State University Press, 1998

Cozzens, Peter, *Shenandoah 1862: Stonewall Jackson's Valley Campaign*, The University of North Carolina Press; Chapel Hill, 2008

Hines, Emilee, *More than Petticoats: Remarkable Virginia Women,* Rowman & Littlefield Publishers, Inc., 2003

Stoddard, Brooke C, and Murphy, Daniel P, *The Everything Civil War Book,* Adams Media; Avon, Massachusetts, 2009

Elizabeth Black

Madison, James H, *Slinging Doughnuts for the Boys: An American Woman in World War II,* Indiana Historical Society Press, Indianapolis, Indiana, 2007

Portraits for the Home Front, Writer/Producer/Director David Solomon, produced by WQED Pittsburgh, PA, 2013

Finding Elizabeth's Soldiers, Writer/Producer/Director David Solomon, produced by WQED Pittsburgh, PA, 2015

Bibliography

Bessie Coleman

Hardesty, Van, *Black Wings*, Harper Collins; New York, New York, 2008

Lady of Cofitachequi

Benson, Lillian P., *Savannah River Meandering,* Otter Bay Books, Baltimore, Maryland, 2016

Rangel, Rodrigo, *Account of the Northern Conquest and Discovery of Hernando DeSoto, Translated by Worth, John E. in The DeSoto Chronicles: The Expedition of Hernando DeSoto In North America in 1539-1543*, Tuscaloosa, University of Alabama, Press, 1993

Spruill, Marjorie Julian, Littlefield, Valinda W, Johnson, Joan Marie, edited by, *South Carolina Women,* University of Georgia Press, Vol. 1; Athens, Georgia, 2009

Susan Butcher

Dolan, Ellen M, *Susan Butcher and the Iditarod Trail,* Walker and Company, New York, 1993

Hamilton, S.L. *Xtreme Races Iditarod,* ABDO Publishing Company, North Mankato, Minnesota, 2013

Stefoff, Rebecca, *Alaska,* Marshall Cavendish Benchmark, New York, 2007

Emma Gatewood

Emblidge, David, edited by, *The Appalachian Trail Reader,* Oxford University Press, New York, New York, 1996

Luxenberg, Larry, *Walking the Appalachian Trail,* Stackpole Books; Mechanicsburg, Pennsylvania, 1994

Montgomery, Ben, *Grandma Gatewood's Walk,* Chicago Review Press, Chicago, Illinois, 2014

The Appalachian Trail: Celebrating America's Hiking Trail, Rizzoli International Publication, Inc.